-17

DEEP CALLS UNTO DEEP

* prayers for
Judy, so
book can
soar
now!
$200.00

* Kelly
minter
2nd Corintheans
" all things new"
1800K

Life Way. Com

Intercessors / America
9:
712-432-0075
Code 1412452#

11-4
Garage Sale
at Judys'

Being
Under
Satens
Yoke

DEEP CALLS UNTO DEEP

In The Song of Solomon

a Bible Study by

JUDY LOKITS

TATE PUBLISHING
AND ENTERPRISES, LLC

This book is designed to provide accurate and authoritative information with regard to the subject matter covered. This information is given with the understanding that neither the author nor Tate Publishing, LLC is engaged in rendering legal, professional advice. Since the details of your situation are fact dependent, you should additionally seek the services of a competent professional.

The opinions expressed by the author are not necessarily those of Tate Publishing, LLC.

Published by Tate Publishing & Enterprises, LLC
127 E. Trade Center Terrace | Mustang, Oklahoma 73064 USA
1.888.361.9473 | www.tatepublishing.com

Tate Publishing is committed to excellence in the publishing industry. The company reflects the philosophy established by the founders, based on Psalm 68:11,

"The Lord gave the word and great was the company of those who published it."

Published in the United States of America
ISBN: 978-1-68333-249-7
1. Religion / Christian Life / General
2. Religion / Biblical Studies / Bible Study Guides
16.07.08

ACKNOWLEDGMENTS

I wish to thank the many who gave me the jump starts when I was stalled. While I have heard and learned much from the many teachings on the Song of Songs over the past decades, I have been most influenced by two pastors who have so much insight into the things of God. My San Diego pastor, Dr. Graham Truscott, and his wife, Pamela, were missionaries in India for more than twenty years before settling in San Diego and starting a church there in the 1980s although they were in demand for their teachings worldwide. Graham's teachings and books, *Here Comes the Bride*, volumes 1 and 2, were especially helpful when I was beginning to explore the bridegroom identity of Christ and what this meant to the church and end-time events.

During the time after my husband's death in 1997, I began to feel the call of the Holy Spirit to a more intimate walk with Jesus. At that time I was given a couple of tapes made at the International House of Prayer in Kansas City and I reveled in the worship music. Years later in Florida, a good friend of mine, also a widow, had found this particular church when she moved to Kansas City and kept telling me about the teachings. The Studies in the Song of Solomon series really caught my ear and heart. Pastor Mike Bickle makes all his teachings freely available online with notes at no cost, and I became a greedy consumer. What I found is that they confirmed what the Holy Spirit was telling me over and over again in my own studies as well as clarifying so many questions I also had about this bridegroom King and His bride. Many of the phrases in his notes have found their way into this book because I could not find a better way to express them.

I cannot leave out the incredibly beautiful and powerful music of Misty Edwards, Gateway Music, and Hillsong, to mention only a few of the artists whose intimate worship led me into the inner chambers of the bridegroom, where I could hear His voice and be changed.

Of the many books I read on the Song of Songs, some were allegories, some shared the author's own personal revelations as they read and studied the love song, and some were commentaries. Where I have quoted passages verbatim, I have attributed these quotes in the text and listed all of them at the end of these acknowledgements.

I am also grateful for my current pastors, Paul and Beth Lavino. They have supported me and trusted me in leadership and teaching roles with their flock and prayed and encouraged me in my endeavors.

Last, but not least, I have been inspired for decades by my very talented and accomplished sister, Kathleen Thompson. Her self-discipline in doing what is necessary to create the multitudes of artistic and inspirational dramatic presentations that mark her international ministry has always prodded me forward. No mountain or valley has ever stopped her. I'm so grateful for her friendship and inspiration in all my efforts.

CONTENTS

AUTHOR'S NOTES

I was desperate to understand why God had allowed me to mess up my life so completely. At sixty-five years old, I had survived an unwanted and tragic (to me) divorce to my marriage with my first great (and only, I thought) love. We had two beautiful children, but after fifteen years, it was over.

A couple of years later, I married again, this time a loving Christian man. But our life for the next twenty years was a constant struggle with legal matters, little or no income, loss of home, and, finally, his struggle with diabetes that left him bedbound for a year until his death. I was fifty-seven years old.

Soon after that, I jumped back into the fire, falling into my third great love. Since he lived in Florida and I in Arizona, I moved to the East Coast to be nearer to him, hoping desperately that we would soon marry. Five years later, I realized this was never going to happen, and we broke it off.

This was followed by the death of my longtime precious dog, Pepper. And then Hurricane Wilma hit south Florida, and the roof of my little house blew off. I was now faced with a total rebuilding, a forced retirement due to the stress of all the chaos surrounding that, and a sense of total bewilderment.

I thought I knew God. He had always been my Heavenly Father and Savior, even as a child, attending Augustana Lutheran Church in Denver regularly, and as an adult, being active in many ways. In my twenties, our church was one of the hosts of the Billy

Graham crusade in Denver, and I volunteered to be a counselor. Being confronted with a more evangelical approach to the gospel, I eagerly asked Jesus to come into my heart. This was a major step into a more intimate knowledge of my Savior and Friend. I became very active in Christian Women's Club (an evangelical outreach to women) and taught a Bible study in my home.

Then as I was facing the cruelties of an unwanted divorce when I was thirty-four, I encountered the move of the Holy Spirit in our city, asked God to baptize me in the Holy Spirit, and entered the joy of living in the power and fiery faith of the Charismatic Movement. It was truly the increase of faith and support of my Charismatic friends that got me through this period and supported me through the difficult years of my second marriage and widowhood.

My move to Florida and the ongoing love relationship with the third love of my life was a huge leap of faith for a woman who had never really been on her own. The Lord blessed me with a good job and, finally, a little house of my own. And I never felt closer to Him than in those years of a frustrating relationship as I constantly sought His will.

Where had I gone wrong? Why was I sixty-five years old, a widow, single, and with no man in my life? My life's desire was to be married to a loving, faithful man, raise a family, and live happily ever after serving the Lord. My children and grandchildren lived across the country, and I saw them only a time or two each year. Why had I moved away just to follow my heart? Had I been wrong?

I felt like Elijah as he ran into the desert, crying out, "I have had enough, Lord. Take my life; I am no better than my ancestors" (1 Kings 19:4, NIV). Just as with Elijah, the Lord had mercy, revealing to me the many and awesome ways He had blessed me, provided for me, protected me, and revealed Himself to me.

However, as with Elijah, I needed to wait for the "gentle whisper" of the ever-persistent Savior. Fortunately, I had the time now and often spent two to four hours a day on my screened-in patio in the balmy Florida mornings, listening and worshipping with my worship music, reading the Word, and writing in my journal. Often, my entries would be questions directed at the Lord only to find that as a thought eased itself into my mind and I wrote it down, it soon became clear that the Holy Spirit (our teacher) was clearly speaking to me. Often, the lyrics of a worship song took me into the presence of the Lord, and I experienced joy, love, peace, and a sense of His actual touch on all my physical senses.

This was when I began to understand the "bridal theology" of the Bible. I began to understand that the Father had chosen me before the beginnings of time and had given me to His Son even then. I had been created to be His bride, to be uniquely made for Him. I found several Bible references to confirm this revelation. When I asked about the other millions who are also part of this bride, He said the same is true of each of them. He also reminded me that in eternity, God is not bound by time, and He is unlimited as to how much we could be together. In eternity, there is no time, and I will enjoy His presence always with no competition from others, who will also have this joy.

As I explored these things over and over during the two years I spent with the "gentle whispers," and verifying them in the Scriptures, I began to identify with this very personal bride of Christ in a real way. I began to understand the bondage I had been in as I thought I could only be truly satisfied with my Prince Charming husband. Jesus showed me that He is the only Prince Charming any of us will ever have, meeting my every need. Even the physical need for tenderness and intimacy can be met by Him, as He fills my spirit with such joy and wonder and security, giving me a sense of complete fulfillment.

Two years later, I began to teach a class for single women in my church, using a manuscript I had written based on my journal and personal experiences. I was then urged to write it as a book and was astonished as I became a published author of *Bouquets from My Beloved*. The truths with which the Lord had blessed me burned in my heart, and I wanted to share them with every woman who also experienced this longing for the perfect bridegroom. I also found that women are not the only ones who face this loneliness, and many men were likewise blessed by the book as they longed for a more intimate knowledge of their Lord.

In 2012, I returned to Phoenix to be closer to my family. My son, his wife, and two children live there, and my daughter, her husband, and daughter lived in San Diego. I found a good church and, after about six months, offered to teach a class using my book. The class was a blessing to us all, and the women wanted to continue, so I again got permission to use my manuscript of this Bible study—*Deep Calls unto Deep*. However, I had only finished the first half, and as it was summer break, we put the rest on hold.

Loving to paint with watercolors, I began teaching watercolor classes and found that my life was very busy—too busy to start writing again to finish the most challenging part of the book. And there it's progress remained.

Once again, two years later—when I was recovering from double knee replacements and impatient with my slow progress and lack of productive activity—the Lord, my Beloved, began to deal with me about completing the *Deep Calls unto Deep* Bible study. There were many reasons I had not done so before. Among them was that I was very busy teaching watercolor classes at three different locations as well as making phone calls to set up appointments for an insurance friend of mine. These were important sources of income and, I believed, provided by the Lord for that reason. I also still hosted a life group at our church.

This is a lot for a seventy-four-year-old woman. I reminded Jesus of these things, and He gently reminded me that He had continued to miraculously provide for me during this lengthy five-month recuperation without the income from my jobs. He also reminded me that fifty years ago I would not have been able to have new knees, and He had given me a great surgeon as well as other medical care. And He gently reminded me how important this Bible study is to those who seek to know Him better.

Then the Holy Spirit began to feed into my thoughts the inspiration that had been missing in order for me to write about the last half of the beautiful Song of Songs. I realized that there is a gentle shift in the story of the Beloved and her Lover. Many commentaries note this and attribute it to the intimate relationship of the now married lovers. I agree. However, these are sensitive passages, causing the reader to often drift into the passions of our own fleshly experiences or on those images we so often see displayed in the modern media, which are hard to avoid. How to appropriately interpret them to a twenty-first-century audience—that had stumped me.

I awoke early one morning with the answer. We, as the corporate bride of Christ, will be gathered to Him at His second coming, seeing Him as He is and becoming like Him (1 John 3:2). This is total intimacy. In Revelation 19, where the wedding supper of the Lamb is spoken of, and in Revelation 21, where the new Jerusalem is described, we again get a hint about the bride, the wife of the Lamb. Until then in our life here on earth, we are the betrothed (promised), bound to Jesus as the bridegroom with an eternal covenant.

Therefore, chapters 5 through 8 in the Song of Songs would seem to speak of our spiritual maturing in our knowledge of Him while here in the flesh as well as our *eternal* love relationship with Jesus. We see ourselves in our imperfect flesh-bound state, living by faith, living in the Spirit, and looking forward to the day when we will experience the fullness of our marriage relationship with Jesus, as promised in the New Testament. This exploded into a whole new understanding of these last four chapters of the Song. And this is the missing link for me in the revelations written about therein.

Although I can only conjecture, as the Bible does not give us any of the details, I believe that this beautiful love song positioned in the absolute middle of the Bible can, at the very least, bring our expectations as the eternal bride of Christ to unknown heights. As with so much of Scripture, it requires the Holy Spirit's help to begin *to know* what the Word is trying to tell us. And this requires us to have a truly seeking heart, one that sacrifices the time and effort to sit at His feet as Mary did. Are you one who will do that?

INTRODUCTION

Most of us have glimpsed the immensity of the kingdom of God and the Spirit's work in ourselves. Just as one chocolate is not enough when the whole box is there beckoning to us, in a spiritual sense, each time our Savior reveals more and more of Himself to us, we long for more. It is in Him that we have life, and in order to have more life, we must begin to know Him more, not more about Him but to know Him more.

There is so much we don't understand. Why did God create the earth? Why man? Why did He give us free choice? We can find a part of the answer in a small book in the center of the Bible, sandwiched between the Old Testament's historical sagas of men of God, the poetic songs of David—a man after God's own heart—and the passionate prophetic promises of grace and its New Testament fulfillment—Jesus.

The Song of Songs is a love story in poetic form, erotic and sensual in parts, because that is how love is. It's a marriage manual for committed love and is utilized for marriage weekends and conferences because it arouses emotions that may have become dull or nonexistent. It speaks of the total commitment of both parties as well as mutual submission.

More importantly, though, the Song is also a spiritual guidebook into the passionate love of God. The bride of Christ is not gender specific. The love story between the bridegroom and His bride uses the format of a female bride and male groom to illustrate the total intimacy available to the believers, both as a corporate entity and as the individual believer when correctly interpreted for that purpose.

It speaks not of a sexual but of a spiritual experience without gender identification, filled with passion and intensity. It has been recognized as such for over three thousand years. Before Jesus's incarnation, God considered Israel as His wife, or in some cases, He labeled her behavior as being adulterous. In the New Testament, Jesus identifies Himself as the bridegroom in numerous places, and John the Baptist recognizes Him in this role, calling himself the friend of the bridegroom. Paul also uses the terms in the allegory to describe the relationship between Christ and the church.

In order to fulfill Jesus's clear explanation about the greatest commandment, we must love Him with all our heart, with all our soul, and with all our mind. This obviously includes our emotions. The language and pictures God chooses describe His love for Israel in the Old Testament and for His church, His bride, and—on the more personal level—the individual believer in the New Testament. The words also speak of the longing for and the passionate love of the believer for her Beloved. This is one of the glorious mysteries of Christ.

The Song of Songs is written in an evocatively passionate style in order to stir our emotional response to the spiritual truths we learn in the rest of the Bible. It is the passionate love of Christ that gives courage to be a martyr, to start a new ministry, to love the unlovable, to heal the sick, and to tirelessly overcome the work of the obstacles put before the spreading of the gospel. It is the fiery love of Jesus that causes us to allow Him to cleanse our hearts and make us holy, lest we disappoint Him with our sin.

The Holy Spirit calls and leads us into this deeper relationship if we are listening. Our betrothal here on earth culminates at the wedding supper of the Lamb, the first event on the program after Jesus's second coming and the gathering of His bride to Himself in her resurrected body.

In this study, we will look at sections of the book, not word for word as in a commentary. There are hundreds of these dating back into Old Testament times and can be very helpful. But the goal in this study is to paint a picture of growth and maturity in our love for God. It takes the Holy Spirit to reveal the truths to us and to help us to respond to the never-ending revelation of God's love for us.

God's name is never mentioned in the text, but His fingerprints are clearly evident to His loved ones.

When we respond to God emotionally,
and we accept His Truth with an act of our will
by the power of the Holy Spirit,
we are changed.

SESSION 1

Our Desire for More

Our life with God is a journey—a journey that starts with His reaching out to us. When we acknowledge our need and recognize our desire to belong to Him, we know that He always responds to that desire. By faith in the Word that tells us of His love for us, our redemption by Him from the penalty of sin, and His promise to give us eternal life, we are made clean in His sight, and He becomes our Savior. But that is just the beginning.

Read the stories noted in our *READ* box and *discuss* the questions below.

> ### READ
> 2 Samuel 11:1–12:26, 1 Kings 19:1–21, Hosea 1 and 2

How do these people respond *emotionally* in their circumstances? How does God respond *emotionally* to us in our struggles?

Discuss with your group.

Our heart, the spiritual dwelling place of God, has a vast and mysterious capacity. It is like a diamond with many facets—beautiful and infinitely valuable. The reason we have deep and diverse emotions is because God does. We are made in His image. Part of His plan is to allow the trials we undergo to trigger those emotions and drive us to Him.

Did you ever wonder why David's sin is so blatantly described when he was supposed to be a man after God's own heart? David's excruciating guilt at knowing he had committed adultery with Bathsheba and conspired to have her husband killed to cover up the unborn child she carried, led him to fasting and a deep repentance experience with the Lord, followed by the ultimate death of their love child. This emotional crisis brought this man to his knees and opened the door of his heart to write many of the incredibly insightful Psalms that minister to us so often. His next son with Bathsheba as his wife was Solomon, the one whom God chose to build the temple. God's love and immense grace are obvious here.

Then we read about Elijah's lapse of courage after he had just dramatically destroyed Queen Jezebel's priests at Mount Carmel. Hearing that there was now a price on his head, he fled and hid—slipping into a fit of fear, self-pity, and unbelief—only to be cared for miraculously there in the wilderness. God then confronted him by the soft whisper of His love, revealing the next great climax in his already exciting ministry.

The prophet Hosea is one of first prophets to understand and allude to the bridal relationship between God and Israel. In the book of Hosea, the prophet is chosen by God to live out his life in such a way as to illustrate His justice, tempered by His passionate grace and love for Israel—His chosen people, His betrothed. This beautiful book reveals a God who has strong and powerful emotions and wants a bride who will respond to His love for her.

In the New Testament, John the Baptist's revelations were the first recorded recognitions of Jesus as the perfect Lamb of God and also as the bridegroom who was coming for His bride (John 3:27–30). You may be surprised at the number of references you will find in your Bible's New Testament concordance and commentary to *bridegroom* and *bride* when referring to Jesus and His redeemed people.

 The last third of this Bible study is a blank JOURNAL.

Each session, you will be asked questions. Write the answers along with the Bible references noting the date in your JOURNAL. Include your personal comments at any point during the lesson. Hopefully, even if you have never "journaled" before, this will help you, step-by-step, to develop the habit and see the value.

Of course, your journal is private. However, there may be times of discussion when you may want to share something you've written.

- When did you come to know Jesus as your Savior?
- List other milestones in your understanding of His love for you.
- Circle words that portray an emotional response on your part.

 Write your answers in your JOURNAL.

Psalm 45 is a key to understanding the primary meaning of the Song and is often quoted in the New Testament as it applies to Christ. The Psalm prophetically describes the wedding procession, the bridegroom, and the bride with no ambiguity.

> Some here see Solomon and Pharaoh's daughter only... they are short-sighted; others see both Solomon and Christ...they are cross-eyed; well-focused spiritual eyes see here Jesus only, or if Solomon be present at all, it must be like those hazy shadows of passers-by which cross the face of the camera, and therefore are dimly traceable upon a photographic landscape. (Charles Spurgeon, *Treasury of David*)

READ
Psalm 45

In the Song, Solomon and the Shulamite, the unnamed principals of the poem, if taken as real people, may deflect from the real purpose of the Song. The story's two leading characters (the bridegroom and the bride) are the Lord Jesus Christ and the church/the individual believer. Variances between the different translations are common due to the literary style of the poem and can cause some confusion as you begin to read. One such feature is the name of the speaker given by the translators at the beginning of a passage. They are not in the original as far as we can tell, and often, credit is given to the bridegroom when others believe that this is a passage spoken by the bride. Therefore, we must rely on the Holy Spirit as He speaks to our heart in these instances.

For the most part, I will refer to Jesus as the *bridegroom* or the *Beloved*, which is in agreement with His words in the Song. The *maiden*, *she*, or *bride* refers to the loved one. The *virgins* or *friends* mentioned along with the daughters of Jerusalem are believers who are either young in their faith or more mature and observing the drama, much like a chorus.

The names and descriptive words used give us real pictures that we can relate to the agrarian lifestyle in the time in which it was written (probably by Solomon himself), understanding that there were no movies, magazines, or other printed pictures with which to describe a beautiful woman or handsome man. The poet's subtle delicacy with which he evokes intense sensuous awareness while avoiding crudeness is a part of the beauty of the Song.

The Song is no ordinary love song. For those of us who are not married, there is a special opportunity to fill that empty place with the most glorious of all bridegrooms, Jesus. For everyone, it sets forth mutual love, communion, fellowship, and delight between the Lord Jesus Christ and the church, in terms of a marriage relationship.

Word Studies that may help you with the language pictures:

Kisses: Psalm 2:12, Psalm 45:2. *Kisses* refers to the extreme desire for intimacy with the Lord, which is derived from His Word, the Word which comes from His mouth.

Perfumes: John 12:3, Luke 23:55–56. Anointing oils were a special way of bestowing value and preciousness.

Chambers: Psalm 27:5, Psalm 91:1. In ancient times, a palace had *outer* courts for feasts and celebrations with the public, *inner* courts for invited guests, and the *inner chambers* where only those who were cherished and loved most warmly were personally invited.

Song of Songs 1:1–8 (niv)

Solomon's Song of Songs

She

Let him kiss me with the kisses of his mouth—
for your love is more delightful than wine.
Pleasing is the fragrance of your perfumes;
your name is like perfume poured out.
No wonder the young women love you!
Take me away with you—let us hurry!

Let the king bring me into his chambers.

Friends

We rejoice and delight in you;
we will praise your love more than wine.

She

How right they are to adore you!
Dark am I, yet lovely,
daughters of Jerusalem,
dark like the tents of Kedar,
like the tent curtains of Solomon.
Do not stare at me because I am dark,
because I am darkened by the sun.
My mother's sons were angry with me
and made me take care of the vineyards;
my own vineyard I had to neglect.
Tell me, you whom I love,
where you graze your flock
and where you rest your sheep at midday.
Why should I be like a veiled woman
beside the flocks of your friends?

Friends

If you do not know, most beautiful of women,
follow the tracks of the sheep
and graze your young goats
by the tents of the shepherds.

Dark am I: She sees herself as not worthy because she knows her true character, blaming it on the past difficulties of her life.

Sheep, goats, shepherd: Often used to describe the church, her leaders, and the Lord's relationship with her.

Vineyard: Isaiah 5:1–4 [dangers of neglecting the vineyard of our spirit]. An oft-used picture of our heart, spirit.

There is an incredibly beautiful plan in the Lord's mind for us—His church, His bride. We see in creation His purposeful planning in nature. The beauty, complexity, order, and extravagance of our world reveal the perfection of His vision for this planet and our environment. As Adam and Eve were created and given complete access to their Creator as well as dominion over their world, they experienced the joy and love of this partnership with their Heavenly Father and Jesus, His Son. They had everything necessary to make their existence a true and complete paradise. They had an intimate and fulfilling relationship with Jesus, their heavenly bridegroom.

Although sin interrupted this beautiful plan, God has never given up on it. In fact, He knew that giving the freedom of choice that was part of the soul of man was risky even though God foresaw the consequences to His most precious created ones—man. Confusing, isn't it?

But then, we have *John 3:16 (NIV), "For God so loved the world that He gave His one and only Son, that whoever believes in Him shall not perish but have eternal life."* He still has His plan. Not only was Jesus sent as Redeemer, but He also saw His believers as His bride. Despite our sense of unworthiness, He's unrelenting in His plan to have us as His Bride, this being the most intimate of relationships. Human marriage is the perfect symbol for this relationship. It is a spiritual bond of total love and commitment.

John the Baptist knew who Jesus was when he said, *"I am not the Messiah, but am sent ahead of Him. The bride belongs to the Bridegroom. The friend who attends the Bridegroom waits and listens for him and is full of joy when he hears the Bridegroom's voice" (John 3:28–29, NIV).*

THIS WEEK

READ
Song of Solomon 1:1–8
Matthew 7:7–8

Use the *Word Studies* provided, and note these and other Holy Spirit revelations in the margins of your Bible. They will be here when you come back to this book in the future.

 Look at this week's entries in your JOURNAL, and add more of your thoughts and insights.

Prayer and Worship

Worship music is the single most important aid to bring us into the presence of the Lord. Do not neglect this aspect of your quiet time.

Get out your iPod, MP3, or CD player and begin to collect some intimate worship music.

Suggestions: "I Love You" (album: *Declare His Name*), "The More I Seek You" (album: *Gateway*), "Relentless" (album: *Relentless-Misty Edwards*), and many, many more. I look for worship music that speaks to God in a personal and intimate way, not necessarily the great congregational hymns.

Look over your answers and comments in your journal. Prayerfully talk to the Lord about them, and don't forget to listen to His comments and replies to your questions to Him. Allow this time to be a special time of sharing with your bridegroom.

Is it difficult for you to respond emotionally especially to the Lord?

Do you feel too unworthy to accept His intimate love?

Is it difficult to hear His quiet voice?

If so, make these things your prayer priorities this week. Remember: Matthew 7:8–9.

SESSION 2

Let's Go a Little Deeper

In review

In our spiritual journey with God, we respond emotionally to His love and care for us. God gave us emotions. He wants us to respond emotionally as well as spiritually. As an example, He often refers to our relationship with Him as a "marriage"—He as the bridegroom, and we as the bride (of Christ). Jesus came in the flesh to pay the "bride price" for His bride and betrothed us to Himself for a future eternity as His wife.

The Song of Songs, a love song, seen spiritually, is a description of this relationship.

Our ability to respond to God's love for us is only as strong as our concept of that love. In short, we need to know who we are to God. This is one of the purposes of the Song of Songs. It is a love letter to us, to you, personally and individually—you!

If you can get past the agrarian and cultural-specific terms that the lovers speak to each other, you will begin to see a most romantic and passionate exchange describing their emotions. Remember, there were no movies, iPods, or electronic books to paint the scenes. It was their surrounding culture and the importance and beauty it spoke to them that were used to express their love and admiration for each other.

The next step for you is to ask the Holy Spirit to begin to translate these messages to your heart to stir your emotions with the revelation of your Beloved's love for you. Then most importantly, tell Him of your love for Him.

> ## READ
> Song of Songs 1:9–2:7, 1 John 4:19, Matthew 22:37–38

Find something that the Lord says to you in the Song of Songs passage above.

How many exchanges between the lovers do you see in this passage?

Why are you seeking to grow in your love for the Lord?

 Record the answers in your JOURNAL. Date your entry.

Use the *Word Studies* below to help you understand the concepts used in the Song.

Mare: A mare would attract great attention among the royal chariot stallions.

Earrings, jewels: Jesus's work in us to beautify us, causing us to seek Him.

Myrrh: (Exodus 30:23, John 19:39–40, Esther 2:12, Psalm 45:8) These speak of Jesus's death and suffering for us.

Henna blossoms: (2 Corinthians 2:14–16) We are the aroma of Christ.

Dove's eyes: (John 1:32) Dove is a symbol of the Holy Spirit, singleness of purpose.

Bed is green: (NAS–couch is luxuriant) A couch speaks of the *rest* of forgiveness and intimacy.

Our house: The house of God, the local church, the dwelling place of God.

Rose of Sharon: Speaks of beauty.

Lily: Speaks of purity.

Song of Songs 1:9–2:7 (NIV)

He

*I liken you, my darling, to a mare
among Pharaoh's chariot horses.*

Your cheeks are beautiful with earrings,
  your neck with strings of jewels.
We will make you earrings of gold,
  studded with silver.

She

While the king was at his table,
  my perfume spread its fragrance.
My beloved is to me a sachet of myrrh
  resting between my breasts.
My beloved is to me a cluster of henna blossoms
  from the vineyards of En Gedi.

He

How beautiful you are, my darling!
  Oh, how beautiful!
  Your eyes are doves.

She

How handsome you are, my beloved!
  Oh, how charming!
  And our bed is verdant.

He

The beams of our house are cedars;
  our rafters are firs.

She

I am a rose of Sharon,
  a lily of the valleys.

He

Like a lily among thorns
*   is my darling among the young women.*

She

Like an apple tree among the trees of the forest
*   is my beloved among the young men.*
I delight to sit in his shade,
*   and his fruit is sweet to my taste.*
Let him lead me to the banquet hall,
*   and let his banner over me be love.*
Strengthen me with raisins,
*   refresh me with apples,*
*   for I am faint with love.*
His left arm is under my head,
*   and his right arm embraces me.*
Daughters of Jerusalem, I charge you by the gazelles and by the
*   does of the field:*
Do not arouse or awaken love
*   until it so desires.*

Amongst thorns: Speaks of our purity amongst the sinful world and unrighteous.

Banner over me: Jesus publicly celebrates His love for us.

Raisins, apples: Our desire for more fruitfulness to express this Love.

Left arm under my head: His unseen protection in the seasons of our spirit.

Right arm embraces me: The sense of His love for us

Do not arouse: Jesus arouses our love and desire for intimacy with Him. This is a response to the Holy Spirit, not our flesh (1 John 4:19).

His Banner over Us Is Love

When Jesus was asked about the greatest commandment, He replied, *"Love the Lord your God with all your heart and with all your soul and with all your mind. This is the first and greatest commandment" (Mat 22:37–38, NIV)*. His greatest desire is for our love. It is the top commandment on His list. It is our first priority.

Our obedience is only as strong as our concept of God's love for us, and our response reflects our perception of how much He loves us. We don't always feel His love. We sometimes feel unworthy. But we are to obey. We are to love Him with all our heart and with all our soul and with all our mind. How can we do that?

The maiden in Song of Solomon's love story knew how. She made mistakes along the way; she was sometimes fearful; she was even sometimes busy. But her Lover always saw her as beautiful, enticing, the desire of His heart.

Do we believe that Jesus sees us this way?

Beautiful

Enticing

The desire of His heart

The best way to find out is to sit under His tree in His shade eating the fruit of His Word and hearing the Words of His heart. When we look up and see His banner over us identifying us by His love for us, we long for more, and we become lovesick for more of His presence. When we discover His unseen protection and receive His unexpected provision, that is His left hand under our head (out of sight). When we perceive His presence with us, touching our senses, that is His right hand of embrace (Song of Songs 2:6).

It is out of this love-exchange that we are able to fulfill the second commandment: loving our neighbor as ourselves. His love in us will flow out, a fountain of love to those around us.

> *I sat down in His shade with great delight, and His fruit was sweet to my taste. (Song of Songs 2:3, NKJV)*

The cross is the only tree that can shade us from the scorching heat of our sin. We only enjoy the shade of God's Word by resting in the shade of Jesus's cross.

Just what is our purpose in God's plan? The church as His bride is being prepared in this age before the second coming. The power of the church, especially in these last days before the Lord returns, will be found in walking in the anointing to love God. This includes the supernatural ability to feel God's love and then to feel love back to God.

> *For the marriage of the Lamb has come, and His wife has made herself ready. (Revelation 19:7, ESV)*

The bride is pictured as a "beautiful rose" and a "pure lily" whose primary life purpose and identity is found in seeking to fully love (rose) and obey (lily) Jesus. The rose is chosen for its beauty and fragrance as the chief of flowers. A lily speaks of purity. The valley speaks of the low and dark places in this fallen world. She lives in purity in the midst of the dark valley of this fallen world. Jesus sees her as His inheritance in the saints.

> *I am the rose of Sharon, and the lily of the valleys. (Song of Songs 2:1, NIV)*

> *That...the Father of glory, may give to you the Spirit of wisdom and of revelation...that you may know...what are the*

riches of His glorious inheritance in the saints. (Ephesians 1:17–18, ESV)

Paul taught the truths of Song 2:1 in teaching that we are betrothed (engaged) to Jesus and live in devotion to Him. Our ultimate destiny in this age is to walk out a lifestyle as His inheritance.

For I betrothed you to one husband, so that to Christ I might present you as a pure virgin. But I am afraid, as the serpent deceived Eve by his craftiness, your minds will be led astray from the simplicity and purity of devotion to Christ. (2 Corinthians 11:2–3, NAS)

 Write in your JOURNAL ways that you have experienced something of what the maiden has shared with us about her heart.

Do you believe that Jesus sees you as beautiful, enticing, the desire of His heart? Write your answer in your JOURNAL.

Discussion: share these insights with your group if you wish.

Come away with me

In Song of Solomon 2:8–15, the Lord comes to us, bounding and leaping, victorious and wanting our fellowship. He has seen the grief, pain, longing in our hearts and wants to turn our attention away from those things and fill us with the hope of the future and our life with Him.

Isaiah 42:9 (NIV) says,

See, the former things have taken place,
and new things I declare;
before they spring into being
I announce them to you.

He invites us to arise from our comfort and security, our fear and sin, to come away with Him to conquer the mountains of this world in total faith and obedience. There is risk there and a need to walk by faith. It is a new place of maturity in our love for Him.

Have you ever been there? Sometimes, we draw back into the clefts of the rock, the hiding places on the mountainside. "I'm saved. I love Him. I do my part. I'm not ready to venture out. That's not my nature." Have you ever said that?

Song of Songs 2:8–15 (NIV)

> *Listen! My beloved!*
>   *Look! Here he comes,*
> *leaping across the mountains,*
>   *bounding over the hills.*
> *My beloved is like a gazelle or a young stag.*
>   *Look! There he stands behind our wall,*
> *gazing through the windows,*
>   *peering through the lattice.*
> *My beloved spoke and said to me,*
>   *"Arise, my darling,*
>   *my beautiful one, come with me.*
> *See! The winter is past;*
>   *the rains are over and gone.*
> *Flowers appear on the earth;*
>   *the season of singing has come,*
> *the cooing of doves*
>   *is heard in our land.*
> *The fig tree forms its early fruit;*
>   *the blossoming vines spread their fragrance.*
> *Arise, come, my darling;*
>   *my beautiful one, come with me".*
>
> *He*
>
> *My dove in the clefts of the rock,*
>   *in the hiding places on the mountainside,*

show me your face,
let me hear your voice;
for your voice is sweet,
and your face is lovely.

She

Catch for us the foxes,
the little foxes
that ruin the vineyards,
our vineyards that are in bloom.

In verse 14, our loving Lord is not daunted or even insulted when we resist. *"Show me your face, let me hear your voice, they are sweet and lovely to me."* He continues to encourage and tell us of His love for us.

In verse 15, she asks Him to help her catch the little foxes that ruin the vineyards (harvest). We need His help to change the small compromises (fear, sinful thoughts, attitudes, words, small yet continual misuse of time and money, unwholesome talk, gossip, unclean thoughts and attitudes). They destroy our intimacy with the Lord.

They may be comfortable, but we must leave them and step out in faith with our Savior, dig deep into our relationship with Him to get free.

READ
John 15:1–8

Jesus in this passage explains that He is the gardener and prunes the branches that cause us to be less than fruitful, that keep us at a distance from Him. We need to understand how loving He is, as He prunes us and releases us from the little *foxes* that ruin our vineyards (fruitfulness). Before we can go on in our quest for intimacy with the Lord, we must understand that this relationship is something to be sought after, longed for, and desired above all else. There is nothing else so valuable. We may be afraid. We may feel unworthy. We may know there are things in our lives that might hinder our journey there.

But His response to us is always one of love and encouragement to trust Him, to know that He desires us. He is calling us to greater maturity in our professed love for Him, greater faith in walking and obeying Him.

> *This is to my Father's glory that you bear much fruit. (John 15:8)*

Meditate on the progression of our maturity in love for Jesus.

Song of Songs 1:13–14: My Beloved is to me.

My initial focus is only upon my spiritual pleasure.

Song Songs 2:16: My beloved is mine, and I am His.

I say He is mine, He belongs to me. Although it is still secondary, I realize that I am also His inheritance.

Song of Songs 6:3: I am my Beloved's, and He is mine.

I change the order. I am putting His agenda first, and my inheritance in Him is still vital but secondary to His inheritance in me (plans for me).

Song of Songs 7:10: I am my Beloved's, and His desire is toward me.

I belong to Him, and what He desires is all I focus on. He owns me entirely. His concerns are what I care about most

Mike Bickel, studies in the Song of Solomon

THIS WEEK

READ
Song of Songs 1:9–2:15; Ephesians 1:18–21

Suggestions for your quiet time with the Lord:

Read out loud the above scriptures to the background of a stirring and passionate piece of music (i.e.: Prokofiev's *Romeo and Juliet*). Let your passions for the Lord be stirred. Use your God-given imagination to see Him as He leaps across the mountains and bounds over the hills, beckoning you to come with Him to a higher place.

Take a walk in a beautiful park or mountain path with your iPod, walkman, or radio tuned to worship music that really stirs you. Stop and listen for His voice.

Get down on your knees, and show Him your list of fears and weaknesses, calling out to Him to "catch the little foxes" and give you the courage to come away with Him.

 Based on these verses, who are you? Write in your JOURNAL and claim them for yourself.

Song of Songs 1:15: _____

Song of Songs 2:1: _____

Song of Songs 2:2: _____

Song of Songs 2:3: _____

Song of Songs 2:4: _____

Song of Songs 2:5: _____

Song of Songs 2:6: _____

Song of Songs 2:10: _____

Song of Songs 2:14: _____

SESSION 3

Seasons in God

Do not arouse or awaken my love until she pleases.

—Song of Solomon 2:7 (NASB)

God has ordained strategic seasons in each person's spiritual life. There are seasons where He desires to establish our heart in new and deep revelations of His heart.

As we have seen in the first two chapters of the Song, the Holy Spirit's agenda for the bride in this season is to awaken lovesickness in her as she goes deeper in the Word (feeding on apples and raisins under the tree and in the banqueting house).

Even John was told to *eat* the scroll in order to understand God's Word in a deep way (Rev. 10:9–11)

Enjoying the loving relationship and expanding revelations of His love, she is enthralled and deeply moved as she encounters the bridegroom while not really knowing much about Him and actually becomes faint with love (lovesick).

In response, He appears to her "leaping across the mountains, bounding over the hills" and passionately inviting her to "come away". In this case, she draws back, not out of rebellion but out of fear and weakness, putting off the leap of faith that her bridegroom is calling her to.

This is a picture of a spiritual season in our life. It is a time when the Holy Spirit draws us and invites us to go with Jesus to the mountain, to live in the high places with Jesus in the extravagant devotion of bridal partnership. What would it mean to live as His bride on this earth and as His wife throughout all eternity?

Song of Songs 2:14–17 (NIV)

He

My dove in the clefts of the rock,
　　in the hiding places on the mountainside,
show me your face,
　　let me hear your voice;
for your voice is sweet,
　　and your face is lovely.
Catch for us the foxes,
　　the little foxes
that ruin the vineyards,
　　our vineyards that are in bloom.

She

My beloved is mine and I am his;
he browses among the lilies.
Until the day breaks
and the shadows flee,
turn, my beloved,
and be like a gazelle
or like a young stag
on the rugged hills.

Psalm 24:3–4 (NASB) says, *"Who may ascend into the hill of the Lord? Or who may stand in His holy place? He who has clean hands and a pure heart."*

If I want to know what it might be like to be the "bride of Christ" in a spiritual sense, then I had best spend a good amount of time in the Sermon on the Mount. Just take some time this week to read Matthew 5, 6, and 7. However, I don't get very far before I realize that what Jesus wants my life to be is far removed from my ability to live that way. There are many foxes to catch in my life. (See Song of Songs 2:15.)

So it follows that to enter into a more intimate and fulfilling relationship with the bridegroom, I must recognize that it is impossible to transform my life in my own strength. In terms of the journey to the high places of God to where He has invited me, I'm overwhelmed with uncertainty and perhaps deep conviction about the state of my impurity and willingness or ability to change.

Love **READ**
Matthew 22:36–39, Psalm 37:4, Jeremiah 29:13, Luke 11:9

What do these verses have in common? *Seek w/ all ♡*
LOVE w/ "
ASK w/ "

"Teacher, which is the great commandment in the Law?" And He said to him, "You shall love the Lord your God with all your heart,

and with all your soul, and with all your mind." This is the great and foremost commandment. The second is like it, "You shall love your neighbor as yourself."

In our journey to greater intimacy, this is where the greatest commandment comes in according to its author, Jesus. As I confess my weaknesses, respond to God's love for me, and love Him back, He changes me, and I can fulfill the second commandment, which is essentially the context of the Sermon on the Mount.

But what about these little foxes? When I am not feeling close to the Lord, I often feel as though I am in a dark place, that the light is missing. Sometimes, it's because He is trying to teach me something. Sometimes, it is because I am resisting a call for purity and obedience in an area of my life.

Sometimes, I, like the bride in our story, am not sure I can follow Him to higher places and surrender my life completely into His hands. It is not long until I realize that being close to Him is more important than anything else. My longing for the sense of His presence is so strong that it compels me to look for, search for, and seek Him with all my heart. I want to throw myself at His feet, confess all my fears and resistance, hold Him, and not let Him go. This is the experience of the bride in our story.

In this passage, the Lord lifts the *sense* of His presence from her heart:

- To *alert* her to the seriousness of her compromise that resists His call
- To *humble* her so as to cause her to be aware of her need for Him
- To *awaken* deep hunger in her for Jesus.

Song of Songs 2:18–3:5 (NIV)

> *All night long on my bed*
> *I looked for the one my heart loves;*
> *I looked for him but did not find him.*

I will get up now and go about the city,
through its streets and squares;
I will search for the one my heart loves.
So I looked for him but did not find him.
The watchmen found me
as they made their rounds in the city.
"Have you seen the one my heart loves?"
Scarcely had I passed them
when I found the one my heart loves.
I held him and would not let him go
till I had brought him to my mother's house,
to the room of the one who conceived me.
Daughters of Jerusalem, I charge you
by the gazelles and by the does of the field:
Do not arouse or awaken love
until it so desires.

Word Studies

Watchmen: Could be the pastors or others in leadership.

Mother's house: House of God (church) where she is taught and fellowships.

Daughters of Jerusalem: Other Christians

Have you ever been hesitant to go deeper in your relationship with the Lord?

Name the little (and big) foxes that ruin the vineyards (your ability to be fruitful in the kingdom of God).

Then once again, the bride *senses* His presence (verse 4). Can you relate?

 Answer and write about it in your JOURNAL.

Of course, He has not gone anywhere. The Lord's response to the maiden's refusal to obey is to lovingly discipline her, causing His manifest presence to be lifted off her heart. He is not angry with her but jealously wants her to share His values as a mature bride, that she might walk in deeper partnership with Him. *"The Spirit...in us yearns jealously" (Jas. 4:5).*

The Holy Spirit speaks here in this strategic season of the bride's heart. His agenda is to awaken lovesickness in her. He charges others around her to not pressure the bride or interfere until she is prepared, until she herself has chosen to respond to the bridegroom's love and invitation to follow Him to higher places.

The Lord has each of us on a tailor-made journey designed for who we are and where we are going. He is the one who draws us and leads us into all truth. It is an ongoing process that will never end until we join Him at His second coming.

Bridegroom or King?

Suddenly, the focus changes with the procession of the King, as He appears in the picture of this love story. Why now? The answer to that question is: it is the knowledge of who He is that helps me know who I am.

The young maiden has just experienced the returning sense of His presence after looking for Him with all her heart. Our Lord cannot resist a seeking heart because He is also our Lover. And the story line of this love song suddenly focuses on who this Lover really is. The bride must see Him in His glory.

It is this revelation that reveals to her who she is. As she sees the royal procession, with the perfumes and incense in the air proceeding it; as the impressive royal guard comes into view, and then the uniquely beautiful palanquin bearing none other than her Beloved, she realizes who He is! This picture, this revelation of His ultimate royalty suddenly opens her heart to the understanding of who she is—the chosen bride of the King of Kings!

He is the bridegroom, and He has come for her! What does this mean for us?

It is difficult to continue deeper into intimacy with the Lord without understanding who He is. Yes, we are:

His children,

His flock,

His friend,

His chosen ones.

However, Jesus also repeatedly referred to those He came to save as His bride, the bride of Christ. Refer to: Matthew 9:15, Mark 2:19, Luke 5:34, John 3:29   *Jesus / Groom*

He is the groom

READ
Psalm 45, Hebrews 1:8–9

Compare these verses with the following passage in the Song of Songs. Do you see the correlations?

Let's look at this awesome procession and beautiful palanquin (a couch or portable chair with curtains used for royal weddings) described in Song of Solomon 3:7–11. (Word Study)

- Perfumed with myrrh and incenses, spices speaks of the fragrance of the knowledge of Him (2 Cor. 2:14)
- Made by the King Himself from the wood of Lebanon, as was the tabernacle—costly, strong, and fragrant.
- Silver pillars (redemption) and gold supports (divine character) protecting the Groom and His bride.
- A seat of purple, speaking of royalty and God's authority which the bride shares.
- Interior tapestries woven with God's love by those who have been transformed by it.
- A valiant guard of sixty warriors speaks of the protection and security enjoyed by the bride.

Song of Songs 3:6–11 (niv)

> *Who is this coming up from the wilderness*
>   *like a column of smoke, made from all the spices of the*
>   *merchant?*
> *Look! It is Solomon's carriage,*
>   *escorted by sixty warriors,*
>   *the noblest of Israel,*
> *all of them wearing the sword,*
>   *all experienced in battle,*
> *each with his sword at his side,*
>   *prepared for the terrors of the night.*
> *King Solomon made for himself the carriage;*
>   *he made it of wood from Lebanon.*
> *Its posts he made of silver,* ~redemption~
>   *its base of gold.* ~divine character~
> *Its seat was upholstered with purple,*
>   *its interior inlaid with love.*
> *Daughters of Jerusalem, come out,*
>   *and look, you daughters of Zion.*
> *Look on King Solomon wearing a crown,*
>   *the crown with which his mother crowned him*
> *on the day of his wedding,*
>   *the day his heart rejoiced.*

The Royal Procession

A big part of our walk with the Lord is receiving by faith the ever-expanding revelation of His nature. This was true of Israel just at it is now. In Exodus, God gradually opened up their eyes to see Him more clearly as He became their great and powerful deliverer and provider, not just their Deity (the unseen God).

He then inserted Himself in their daily lives with the Law, giving them wise and healthy ways to live and enjoy His blessings.

David and the prophets—especially Isaiah, Jeremiah, and Hosea—had glimpses of His plan to redeem His chosen people (including us) and to prepare them to be His eternal companion and bride.

Then with His incarnation as the Messiah and His immeasurable act of love in taking on Himself the sin of His intended bride, a huge revelation opened up to us. It is the work of the Holy Spirit to lead us into all *truth*. And it is our work to respond to this truth in faith.

As we step out onto the water as Peter did, the Lord reaches out His hand and leads us into a deeper walk in faith.

Ephesians 2:6 says, *"Raised us up together, and made us sit together in the heavenly places in Christ."*

How does this verse relate to the above passage? How does it relate to you?

 Journal about it.

Understanding this revelation of the royal and divine bridegroom causes us to grow in love, both in feeling loved and in having the power to love back. We are most secure when God's affections are understood. We are then willing to allow Him to conform us to His image.

This becomes our greatest goal.

THIS WEEK

READ again in your Bible Song of Songs 2:14–17, 3:1–11

Jot down little notes in the margins of your Bible as the Holy Spirit reveals what the verses mean.

 As you reread this lesson, *add* these questions and answers to your JOURNAL entries:

- Are you struggling, not sure you want to go deeper, to pay the cost of your independence?
- Write a prayer to your bridegroom about it. Also, ask your leader or pastor for help if you need more advice.
- Write out the various characteristics (truths) of the King that speak to you about Jesus as your King, Savior, bridegroom (i.e.: King—crowned, loving, majestic, eternal, all powerful, etc.)
- What parts of the royal procession speak to you? Why?
- Write out a list of these parts (i.e.: valiant guard, sharing the royal authority seat of the King) and use them in your prayer life. These are our weapons in warfare.

As the bridegroom rejoices over the bride,
so shall your God rejoice over you.

—*Isaiah 62:5 (ESV)*

SESSION 4

Going Deeper

The picture of the bridegroom and His bride is the perfect way to describe the all-fulfilling relationship that grows in each of us as we seek to know Him more.

It is important that we do not lose the entire picture of the story that is being told here in the Song of Songs. God has inserted this beautiful book in the middle of the Bible as an illustration of the passionate love of our God for His people. We often get so busy "being a Christian" that we lose the passion and romance of who He is and who we are. Men as well as women need to get in touch with the fiery love spoken of here.

Review the story.

The Lord has captured the heart of His bride, and she is love-sick for Him. He loves her and calls her to come away with Him. The bride falters, unsure of herself, and loses the sense of His presence. He again makes His presence known, and she renews her passion for Him, sharing her love for Him with her church, friends, and family.

Then the picture changes. We hear the Holy Spirit calling her to view the procession of the King. Preceded with fragrant aromas and incense, the King is bringing the wedding palanquin to meet His bride and take her to the wedding. It is guarded by sixty valiant warriors. He is the bridegroom coming for His bride!

On the journey to the wedding feast, the Lord showers her with words of love, telling her who she is, how He sees her, through the eyes of the Creator with His perfect design and with the heart of the Savior who has washed her with the water of the Word. He uses agrarian terms and descriptions to give her a picture of what He sees, terms that would have great meaning and value in that simple lifestyle and community of the time in which the Song was written. He reminds her of His sacrifice on the mountain of myrrh and frankincense (His crucifixion), and she now comprehends the depth of the transformation He has given her because of His love for her.

He then asks her to join Him and face the unknown with Him, trusting herself totally to His care, as she sheds the old skin of her flesh like a butterfly and lives in the Spirit, guided by His truth and nurtured by the comprehension of His passionate love for Her.

Richard Brooks writes in his book, *Song of Songs*, "It is important to understand that behind the various bodily parts that are being mentioned in these verses, it is of spiritual beauty that we are to learn, 'the inner man' (Eph. 3:16), 'the hidden person of the heart'

(1 Pet. 3:4), the adorning 'the doctrine of God our Saviour in all
things' (Tit. 2:10). 'For the Lord does not see as man sees; for man
looks at the outward appearance, but the Lord looks at the heart'
(1 Sam. 16:7)." He adds, "Here it is the beauty of modesty, humil-
ity, tenderness, and chastity that is intended—the very opposite of
worldly pride, gaudiness, or any brash or coarse flaunting of self."

As you read the Song verses, keep this in mind.

The following are character traits that God wants to develop
in His bride:

- Dove's eyes—spiritual insight (Ephesians 1:18), purity
  and loyalty (Holy Spirit pictured as a dove)
- Hair like a flock of goats—dedication to God (Nasserite's
  hair) (woman's hair [1 Corinthians 11:5, 6, 15]); the
  stately walk of a goat (Proverbs 30:29–31)
- Teeth like shorn sheep—the ability to chew on the meat
  of the Word
- Lips like a strand of scarlet—they bring redemption to
  others (Rahab's scarlet strand [Joshua 2:21]), blood of
  calves and scarlet wool used by Moses to sprinkle the
  people (Hebrews 9:19)
- Temples veiled—can be translated *cheeks* which reveal
  one's emotions, red (like a piece of pomegranate) speaks
  of one sensitive to shameful things (blushing), a hidden
  life of modesty and tenderness.
- Neck like David's tower—strong and high towers indi-
  cate a resolute will to obey God and ability to use God's
  spiritual weapons
- Breasts like two fawns—the ability to feed and nurture
  others, feeding among the lilies speaks of purity

- Mountain of myrrh—speaks of Jesus's sacrifice (myrrh used for burial), the commitment to deny ourselves and take up our cross (Luke 9: 23–26)
- Hill of frankincense–Speaks of prayer, Psalm 141:2, Revelation 5:8, our prayer empowers our heart to embrace the cross with self-denial and spiritual warfare

- North and South winds—Speaks of the difficult sufferings (north) and joyous (south) times of blessing

Song of Songs 4:1–11 (NIV)

He

How beautiful you are, my darling!
  Oh, how beautiful!
    Your eyes behind your veil are doves.
Your hair is like a flock of goats
    descending from the hills of Gilead.
Your teeth are like a flock of sheep just shorn,
    coming up from the washing.
Each has its twin;
    not one of them is alone.
Your lips are like a scarlet ribbon;
    your mouth is lovely.
Your temples behind your veil
    are like the halves of a pomegranate.
Your neck is like the tower of David,
    built with courses of stone;
on it hang a thousand shields,
    all of them shields of warriors.
Your breasts are like two fawns,
    like twin fawns of a gazelle

that browse among the lilies.
Until the day breaks
  and the shadows flee,
I will go to the mountain of myrrh
  and to the hill of incense.
You are altogether beautiful, my darling;
  there is no flaw in you.

Come with me from Lebanon, my bride,
  come with me from Lebanon.

Descend from the crest of Amana,
  from the top of Senir, the summit of Hermon,
from the lions' dens
  and the mountain haunts of leopards.

You have stolen my heart, my sister, my bride;
  you have stolen my heart
with one glance of your eyes,
  with one jewel of your necklace.
How delightful is your love, my sister, my bride!
  How much more pleasing is your love than wine,
and the fragrance of your perfume
  more than any spice!
Your lips drop sweetness as the honeycomb, my bride;
  milk and honey are under your tongue.
The fragrance of your garments
  is like the fragrance of Lebanon.

READ
Ephesians 5:25–27, Psalms 18:35, Philippians 2:13

What do the above verses have in common?

God's work in God's love
us. 4 us.

Write your answer to the above question in your JOURNAL. Discuss with your group.

The story of the King and His bride speaks to us on so many levels.

- The joy of finding our Savior and responding to His love through salvation and the filling of His Spirit
- The revelation of a deeper and more filling relationship that brings healing and restoration of the heart for those who have suffered great loss (a normal part of our Christian walk)
- The indescribable experience of getting to know the heart of our Lover, to share life with Him, moment by moment, and responding in complete obedience
- The joy and hope of total union with Him in eternity, becoming like Him and seeing and touching Him face-to-face, the consummation of our longed for dreams

The beautiful and sensual description of our love for Christ is not a story of erotic *fleshly* passion. It is the story of a fiery *spiritual union* that stirs our entire being, bringing healing, restoration, and hope for even more.

Name three Biblical characters who experienced this pattern of spiritual growth in their lives (for example: Moses, David, Ruth, Esther, the disciples, Peter, Paul, Mary Magdalene, Mary and Martha, Mary, the mother of Jesus)

 Write in your JOURNAL about the results of the growth in each of these three example's life.

The agrarian terms of the bride's character and their Biblical interpretations. (There are dozens of meanings given to these terms from numerous Bible commentaries.) Have you found any others besides these?

 Write in your JOURNAL how you feel *you* compare with this description.

Note: Satan's number one job is to accuse and distort our perception of our *own* spiritual growth.

In what ways does he do that? *just never good enough*

How can you protect yourself from his lies? Discuss with your group.

Garden locked up: Our heart, the most secret place of our soul.

Choice fruits: Look up in your Bible commentary for various interpretations of these fruits and spices.
Our garden is watered by the living water of the Spirit.
 Our garden is made beautiful and intimate by the presence of Jesus and His Spirit.

Let's continue with the bridegroom's love language to his bride. *Song of Songs 4:12–16, 5:1 (niv)*

> *You are a garden locked up, my sister, my bride;*
> *you are a spring enclosed, a sealed fountain.*
> *Your plants are an orchard of pomegranates with choice fruits,*
> *nard and saffron,*
> *calamus and cinnamon,*
> *with every kind of incense tree,*
> *with myrrh and aloes*
> *and all the finest spices.*
> *You are a garden fountain,*

a well of flowing water
streaming down from Lebanon.

She

Awake, north wind,
and come, south wind!
Blow on my garden,
that its fragrance may spread everywhere.
Let my beloved come into his garden
and taste its choice fruits.

He

5 I have come into my garden, my sister, my bride;
I have gathered my myrrh with my spice.
I have eaten my honeycomb and my honey;
I have drunk my wine and my milk.

If you saw the beautiful movie *The Secret Garden*, you may remember the story of a dead and untended garden secreted behind vine covered walls. The garden was on an estate where the young heir was also seriously ailing. When friends discovered the vast garden and began to love it back into life, they brought the boy there. He also came to life.

Our heart contains a secret garden—our spirit. Until we are born again, our garden is also dead. But when we give our heart to Jesus and accept His forgiveness and righteousness, our spirit is given life—His Life. As we, like the children in the movie, spend time there, the beauty of that garden is manifested in our life.

The garden paintings of Thomas Kinkaid are beautiful images of gardens filled with light. They give us a glimpse of the special place in our heart where Jesus longs to spend intimate time with us.

God's love for us is not just a static constant in our lives. He is the Creator. The garden is the place of His creation in us where the life of God pollinates the seeds of faith within us to bring forth fruit.

 List terms Jesus uses to describe His bride in this love song to her in your JOURNAL. What do you believe they mean?

Do you believe He can say that to you? Write about that.

Discuss with your group.

The Garden of Eden

Genesis 1:27–31 tells us about the culmination of six days of creation. If we look closely, we can grasp some of the vision the Trinity had for earth.

- A paradise of beauty and provision
- A place of intimate communication between God and man
- A place of fruitfulness in nature, the plants, and animals
- A partnership of dominion over this paradise
- A place of perfect love and fulfillment

And then the black stain of sin placed this beautiful plan on hold.

For now, that place can only be experienced spiritually. We have yet to see this plan's complete picture. It awaits us in eternity after Jesus returns for His bride. But the Bible speaks often of gardens and fruitfulness and the unseen gardener. Could it be that our spiritual garden, basking in the love of the bridegroom, is a spiritual fulfillment of the original plan for Eden?

It is this inner garden of our heart that contains the seeds implanted by the Word. These seeds germinate and result in the fruitfulness that characterizes the bride of Christ. His love and our surrender to that love in humble obedience bring forth the ripe fruit producing fragrant perfumes and spices. The living water which comes from the indwelling Holy Spirit becomes a spring enclosed, a well of flowing water. We are becoming filled with fruit.

Look up these words or phrases in your Bible's concordance:
Garden or gardener
Vineyard
Fruitful or fruitfulness

READ
Luke 8:11–15, John 7:37–38, 2 Corinthians 2:14–16

 How do these verses relate to our Christian life? Write about it in your JOURNAL.

Awake, North Wind, and Come, South Wind!

One of the hallmarks of maturity in our walk with the Lord is the awareness of our inability to be as fruitful and effective as we would like to be. We long to love Him back and live lives of perfect obedience, only to find ourselves staring at our failures.

The Lord also sees our longing heart and pleading cries and He responds by telling us of our beauty and perfection in His righteousness and He calls us away to a place of greater surrender...the surrender of the control of our life. His love draws us like honey draws a bee.

In Song of Solomon 4:16 the bride, now confident in God's goodness, prays for both the north winds of adversity (bringing testing and difficulty) and the south winds of blessings (to mature her).

She prays for more fruitfulness that might spread abroad. And she prays for her Lover to come into her garden, which is closed to all others. She wants to share the deep things of her life with Him and she wants Him to share the mysteries of His Life with her. This place of beauty and fulfillment is the most inner part of her heart, a place of total surrender.

And Jesus waits no longer! As her Bridegroom He immediately takes ownership (Song 5:1). Nine times He says "My" when referring to her garden. He gathers what the Spirit has worked through her life, feasting on the fruit of a mature bride (His glory). He celebrates her love for Him and is delighted and glorified by it. And He invites His corporate church to all experience this deep love.

This is the turning point in the song. Instead of Him being *her inheritance*, she now sees herself as *His inheritance*. (Ephesians 1:18)

THIS WEEK

Using Your Imagination

God has given us this beautiful gift of imagination in order to picture the things we hear and read about. If you haven't tried to close your eyes and allow the Holy Spirit to take you to this beautiful garden, it is now time to do so.

In your personal worship, hopefully with music, visualize the Lord and yourself walking and talking there, sitting and resting by a stream or lying in the grass watching the clouds go by as you share the deep things of your heart and you listen as He speaks of the mysteries of His heart.

Jesus often shared these kinds of experiences with others in the gospels, why not you?

If you have been a part of this Bible study, you have most likely experienced one or more of these levels in your growth in maturity (see page 60). Often, we go forward and slip back for a time until the Holy Spirit calls us once again to climb higher.

 Write about it in your JOURNAL.

For now we see only a reflection as in a mirror; then we shall see face to face. Now I know in part; then I shall know fully, even as I am fully known.

—1 Corinthians 13:12–13 (NIV)

Define your Garden + visit daily.

SESSION 5

Seeking His Face

The Cry of the Bride

*The LORD bless you and keep you; the LORD make his
face to shine upon you and be gracious to you;
The LORD lift up his countenance upon you and give you peace.*

—Numbers 6:24–26 (NKJV)

What happens in the garden?

Some might wonder what happens when we invite the Lord to "come into my garden." With the help of our Holy Spirit's inspired imagination, the Word, music, and the beauties of nature, we can often see ourselves with Jesus in a paradise of beauty and peace. Or we might feel a real sense of peace and love in a hazy environment filled with His presence. Others see themselves walking with Jesus along a beautiful beach or in a meadow filled with flowers beside a quiet stream, gliding arm in arm with Him ice skating or dancing in a beautiful palace ballroom or even riding horses across a rolling countryside. Our experiences are all different and very unique.

Mostly, we long for His companionship, His intimate words of love, and the acknowledgement that we are cherished and uniquely beautiful to Him. We know that we desperately need Him and we want to love Him back.

Read Moses's account of his face-to-face encounters with God.

The Tent of Meeting

Now Moses used to take the tent and pitch it outside the camp, far off from the camp, and he called it the tent of meeting. And everyone who sought the Lord would go out to the tent of meeting, which was outside the camp. Whenever Moses went out to the tent, all the people would rise up, and each would stand at his tent door, and watch Moses until he had gone into the tent. When Moses entered the tent, the pillar of cloud would descend and stand at the entrance of the tent, and the Lord would speak with Moses. And when all the people saw the pillar of cloud standing at the entrance of the tent, all the people would rise up and worship, each at his tent door. Thus the Lord used to speak to Moses face to face, as a man speaks to his friend. (Exodus 33:7–11, ESV)

*After receiving the Law-Face to face with God...Whenever
Moses went in before the Lord to speak with Him, he would
remove the veil, until he came out. And when he came out and
told the people of Israel what he was commanded, the people of
Israel would see the face of Moses, that the skin of Moses' face
was shining. And Moses would put the veil over his face again,
until he went in to speak with Him. (Exodus 34:34–35)*

Moses wore a veil because he did not want the Israelites to see
the glory of God fading from his face.

When the glory of God lights up our face (spiritually) because
we have encountered Him, we no longer need to put a veil over
our face because He is always in our hearts, abiding in the garden,
perpetuating the glow.

*For God, who said, "Let light shine out of darkness," made his
light shine in our hearts to give us the light of the knowledge
of God's glory displayed in the face of Christ.*

—2 Corinthians 4:6 (NIV)

Dividing the *Song of Songs* in the middle is the interlude in
the garden, which encompasses one of the beautiful mysteries of
the Bible. It speaks of the preparation of the bride for the most
intimate of relationships with her lover and his passionate answer
as he is moved by her absolute love and trust in him.

Just as the Old Testament and the New Testament differ
in their descriptions of the relationship between Israel (or the
church) and their God, the two halves of the Song also describe
a different experience between the lovers.

The Old Testament and the first half of the Song tell the stories of an immature love relationship hindered by fear, unbelief,
and sin. However, the New Testament reveals the Lord's plan to
deliver His bride from her old life by going to the "mountains of
myrrh" at the cross to redeem her before coming back to claim
her as His bride.

In the Song of Solomon following her lover's visit to the "mountains of myrrh," the bride invites him into her most secret place—her garden. She has left behind her former life and embraced the workings of the adversities as well as the blessings of trust and faith.

Here in the garden, as in life in the Holy Spirit, the beloved bride enters into the beginnings of a totally committed, marriage-type of relationship. This is no longer a flirtation or a casual affair. **What does the Lord do for us in the garden?**

Let's go back to Song of Songs 4:9–15. It is the revelation of who we are that changes us. That revelation comes when we are in His presence, often in the garden. It is in the knowing that He passionately loves us and longs for our presence as well that we are healed emotionally.

Using the words of the Song, write down in your JOURNAL your interpretation of the ways that you please your bridegroom, Jesus.

What words does your bridegroom use to describe who you are? *Song of Songs 4:9–5:1 (NIV)*

> *You have stolen my heart, my sister, my bride;*
> *you have stolen my heart*
> *with one glance of your eyes,*
> *with one jewel of your necklace.*
> *How delightful is your love, my sister, my bride!*
> *How much more pleasing is your love than wine,*
> *and the fragrance of your perfume*
> *more than any spice!*
> *Your lips drop sweetness as the honeycomb, my bride;*
> *milk and honey are under your tongue.*
> *The fragrance of your garments*
> *is like the fragrance of Lebanon.*

> *You are a garden locked up, my sister, my bride;*
>   *you are a spring enclosed, a sealed fountain.*
> *Your plants are an orchard of pomegranates*
>   *with choice fruits,*
>   *with henna and nard,*
>   *nard and saffron,*
>   *calamus and cinnamon,*
>   *with every kind of incense tree,*
>   *with myrrh and aloes*
>   *and all the finest spices.*
> *You are a garden fountain,*
>   *a well of flowing water*
> *streaming down from Lebanon.*

Look up these words in your Bible concordance or a Bible dictionary for some help in various interpretations of the descriptive words. Ask the Holy Spirit to lead you and guide you as you study these.

Amend your answer to your first interpretation if necessary.

> *Those who look to Him are radiant, and*
> *their faces shall never be ashamed.*
>
> —Psalm 34:5 (ESV)

Note for interpretation of *myrrh*: Frankincense and myrrh were widely available when the Magi visited the baby Jesus and would have been considered practical gifts with many uses. The expensive resins were symbolic as well. Frankincense, which was often burned, symbolized prayer rising to the heavens like smoke while myrrh, which was often used for burials, symbolized death. Accordingly, a mixture of wine and myrrh would be offered to Jesus during His crucifixion.

While, in truth, all this happens to some extent when we receive Jesus Christ as our Savior and we are born again, it is also true that we are constantly being called by Jesus to know Him better, to know and understand His heart, and to understand the true nature of our relationship with Him. After all, we are His creation.

As a part of the triune God, He is far more than any one aspect of His nature. We can never expect to know much more if we do not answer His invitation to explore our relationship with Him.

It is His love for us that draws us to do so. His love is the only thing that truly satisfies, and a little of that love is never enough.

It is our full surrender and need for Him that draws us upward into His arms of passion and the revelation of how deep that love is.

Song of Solomon 4:16 (NIV)

She

Awake, north wind,
*   and come, south wind!*
Blow on my garden,
*   that its fragrance may spread everywhere. Let my beloved*
*   come into his garden*
*   and taste its choice fruits.*

In this one verse (above), we overhear the bride in the deepest of conversations. She invites the north winds of adversity and south winds of blessing to come into her life. She does this now understanding that trials, or following her lover to the mountains of myrrh while terrifying, allows her to grow in her relationship with him. She invites her bridegroom into her garden—the most private place of her heart—trusting Him in her longing for His presence.

Note that she must ask first. The clear lesson here is that if we wish to go on in God—to really get to know Him, to come into that place of real intimacy with the Creator of us—that door has to be opened by us. ✳ *We must ask.*

READ
Psalm 73:25–26, Revelation 3:20

How do these verses relate to the bride's decision?

What do we do in the garden?

1. First of all, carve out at least an hour where you can be protected from interruptions. This sacrifice of your time is pleasing to the Lord and will be greatly rewarding to you.

2. Enter His gates with thanksgiving and His courts with praise (Psalm 100:4). The outer courtyard of a king was generally for the common people, and from there, an invited guest would enter another gate to the King's chambers. However, only the most intimate of friends or family were ever invited into the inner chambers of the King. The garden spoken of in the Song of Songs is also the inner chambers of the King Jesus's dwelling place in us. One of the most rewarding ways to enter this private place is through thanksgiving, praise, and worship. Use recorded music or make your own, and let the worship open your heart.

   If you do not have recorded music available, open to one of the Psalms listed on the next page. (THIS WEEK, page 78) Say or sing it to the Lord.

3. Ask the Lord to cover your consciousness and imagination with the Holy Spirit, leading you into His truth and protecting you from deception. Then trust Him to do it. ✳

4. Depending on your own personal and unique need at that time, read the Word, perhaps using a favorite daily devotional or a scripture that has come to your mind.

5. Give over this time to the Holy Spirit to lead you into truth. Begin a conversation with the Lord. He is your Betrothed and wants this to be a two-way encounter.

6. Listen for His answers to your questions. This changes this time from a devotional period to a more intimate conversation with the Lord. Expect Him to enter into the conversation. It may take a while for you to recognize His voice. At first, you may think it is a thought of your own but ask another question and listen again. Don't let the enemy of doubt come in and rob you of this blessing. Keep trying.

    Writing in your journal in a conversational style (Q&A with the Lord) is a great way to expand this conversation.

7. Relax at His feet, lay your head on His shoulder. Allow yourself to feel His presence as it washes you and heals you and refreshes you (Romans 8:11).

8. Be obedient to anything He asks of you, knowing that He will be there with you. Acknowledge His work in your heart, and yield to Him.

    Enjoy!

Jesus Calling by Sara Young is a helpful and inspiring daily devotional. According to the author, the daily entries are Holy Spirit breathed to her and were recorded in her journals.

On January 23, it reads this way:

> Let My love enfold you in the radiance of My Glory. Sit still in the light of My Presence, and receive My Peace. These quiet moments with Me transcend time, accomplishing far more than you can imagine. Bring Me the sacrifice of your time, and watch to see how abundantly I bless you and your loved ones.
>
> Through the intimacy of our relationship, you are being transformed from the inside out. As you keep your

focus on Me, I form you into the one I desire you to be. Your part is to yield to My creative work in you, neither resisting it nor trying to speed it up. Enjoy the tempo of a God-breathed life by letting Me set the pace. Hold My hand in childlike trust, and the way before you will open up step-by-step.

In the Garden

Song of Solomon 5:1 (NKJV)

The Beloved

I have come to my garden, my sister, my spouse;
I have gathered my myrrh with my spice;
I have eaten my honeycomb with my honey;
I have drunk my wine with my milk.

(To His Friends)

Eat, O friends!
Drink, yes, drink deeply,
O beloved ones!

The bridegroom takes ownership, full possession of her life—His inheritance (Ephesians 1:18).

- Verse 1a: He comes into His garden.
- Verse 1b: He gathers His myrrh (our embrace of the cross) with His spice (the grace imparted in our life).
- Verse 1c: He feasts on the fruit (of the Spirit) evident in our life.
- Verse 1d: He enjoys and celebrates our love for Him.

 Write in your JOURNAL the ways in which you are growing in your knowledge of Jesus as your bridegroom.

THIS WEEK

Make time to visit the garden with your bridegroom.

It is a deep mystery—this transference of His light and life into us. Do not try to figure it out.

Glorify Him by delighting in Him and being with Him.

Experience the joy of being transformed and refreshed in His presence.

Use these in your praise and worship:

Psalm 5, 8, 18, 19, 24, 30, 33, 34, 45, 46, 67, 86, 91, 92, 95–101, 103–106, 111, 118, 138, 139, 145–150

SESSION 6

Abiding with Him

Abide in Me, and I in you. As the branch cannot bear fruit of itself, unless it abides in the vine, neither can you, unless you abide in Me.

—John 15:4 (NKJV)

This is the turning place in the Song of Songs. While the first four chapters are all about her inheritance in Him, exploring her love for Him and what it brings to her, the last four chapters focus on Jesus's inheritance in His bride. She lives in Him, and He enjoys (is ravished by) His inheritance in her. He has taken ownership of her as she surrenders and opens herself to Him. She is His desire.

As she lives her life, she is often aware of His voice, saying, "Open for Me, My sister, My love, My dove, My perfect one, for My head is covered with dew, My locks with the drops of the night." He is reminding her of His suffering night in Gethsemane when He chose His Father's will over His own weak flesh, when He chose her. He is calling her to do the same, to follow Him, even sharing in His sufferings (Phil. 3:10), to open her heart to experience new depths in Him (Rev. 3:20).

This experience of hearing His voice in both the north winds of adversity and the south winds of blessing is fundamental to a mature life of abiding in Him.

Song of Solomon 5:2–8 (esv)

> *She*

> *I slept, but my heart was awake.*
> *A sound! My beloved is knocking.*
> *"Open to me, my sister, my love,*
>   *my dove, my perfect one,*
> *for my head is wet with dew,*
>   *my locks with the drops of the night."*
> *I had put off my garment;*
>   *how could I put it on?*
> *I had bathed my feet;*
>   *how could I soil them?*
> *My beloved put his hand to the latch,*
>   *and my heart was thrilled within me.*
> *I arose to open to my beloved,*
>   *and my hands dripped with myrrh,*
> *my fingers with liquid myrrh,*
>   *on the handles of the bolt. I opened to my beloved,*

but my beloved had turned and gone.
My soul failed me when he spoke.
I sought him, but found him not;
   I called him, but he gave no answer.
The watchmen found me
   as they went about in the city;
they beat me, they bruised me,
   they took away my veil,
     those watchmen of the walls.
I adjure you, O daughters of Jerusalem,
   if you find my beloved,
that you tell him
   I am sick with love.

These beautiful verses should describe our life with the Lord as we "abide with Him." We have renounced our sin, we live in the power of His cleansing blood. And when we hear Him speaking to us, we yearn for Him. We rush to encounter Him again and to be with Him.

In the Song, the bride hears His call, responds by refusing to go back to her old ways, by putting on her old garment of sin and walking in it. She yearns to be with Him again no matter where it leads. She rises to open for her Beloved.

Question: why all this talk about myrrh?

The bride's hands and fingers drip with myrrh, speaking of death to self and her ongoing working faith to follow in obedience as she accompanies her Husband in His love and ministry for the world.

READ

Isaiah 61:10, Isaiah 64:6, Romans 13:14, John 13:6–11

These verses speak of taking off our filthy rags of sin and daily washing our feet—spiritual cleansing.

The lover in our story prepares His bride for the coming challenges to her faith by calling her four names of endearment. And so the Lord empowers us with tender words that speak of different facets of her relationship with Him in preparation for our life in intimate partnership with Him.

 When the Lover called out to His bride in verse 2, what are the four different names that He called her?

1. My _____
2. My _____
3. My _____
4. My _____

Record in your JOURNAL.
This is how He speaks of you.
- He reminds her that (1) He identifies with her humanity, enduring its sufferings and joys for her sake (Mk. 3:34, Heb. 2:11).
- His next name (2) for her stirs up the strongest of emotions as it reminds her of His grace in choosing her (Jn. 17:26, Eph. 5:25).
- The dove (3) speaks of the singleness of mind and loyalty which now directs her life (Heb. 12:2).
- Perfect one (4), in the sense that her intentions are to be obedient, describes her maturity (Eph. 5:27).

As we too hear these words of Jesus, they cause us to trust in Him. We know He loves us and desires us more than we long for Him. As the bride in the Song quickly rises with a pounding heart to open to her lover, we too must not hesitate to respond to His call to our heart to come away and spend time with Him. There are times, as with the bride, when we rush to Him, but we do not sense His presence. However, a mark of our maturity is the ability to not waver in the understanding of our mutual love for each other and to go forth in faith. Jesus promised to never leave us or forsake us; however, He sometimes tests our faith in order to bring it to maturity by withdrawing His discernible presence. This is not because of our disobedience, as in Song 3:1–2, or an attack of the devil. He is often drawing out the yearning of our heart for Him, reminding us of our love for Him. We must remember, *"His banner over me is love" (Song of Songs 2:4, NASB).*

Even though we may be abused or misunderstood for our intense relationship with Jesus, our testimony to others is, "I am lovesick." We continue to share with others His love and life within us regardless of their reaction or the difficulties around us. We read His Word reminding ourselves of His promises. We worship Him and obey Him, walking in this test of faith.

Questions and Answers

How is your beloved better than others,
most beautiful of women?
Where has your lover gone, most beautiful of
women (Song of Songs 5:9, 6:1)?

Perhaps, we should ask the bride's friends (immature Christians) why they find her so beautiful. They see that she is lovesick for her bridegroom. Even though He does not appear to be with her, yet she does not complain. It is our deep love for Jesus that makes us beautiful, not our wisdom or power. It is our wholehearted devotion and faith in Him that attracts others to us. They want to know all about this One we love. Her intimate knowledge of Him is evident in her reply to her friends.

At all times, we must be able to tell others about our Lord, our Husband—Jesus. Our relationship with Him is so rich that it must be shared, and when we do, He often reveals Himself in our sharing. He hasn't left us after all!

Suggestions for describing the Lord:

Radiant and ruddy: glory of God, human form
His head: sovereign, leader
His hair: virile, effective strength
His eyes: absolutely unwavering, wise, understanding
His cheeks: delightful emotions
His lips, His words: holy, unique, personal
His arms/hands: divine activity
His body: unequaled in beauty/compassion
His legs: majestic, holding all things together
His appearance: strength imparted to us
His mouth: the sweetness of His words

Song of Songs 5:9–16 (NIV)

Friends

How is your beloved better than others,
    most beautiful of women?
How is your beloved better than others,
    that you so charge us?

She

My beloved is radiant and ruddy,
    outstanding among ten thousand.
His head is purest gold;
    his hair is wavy
    and black as a raven.
His eyes are like doves

by the water streams, washed in milk,   mounted like jewels.
His cheeks are like beds of spice
* yielding perfume.*
His lips are like lilies
* dripping with myrrh.*
His arms are rods of gold
* set with topaz.*
His body is like polished ivory
* decorated with lapis lazuli.*
His legs are pillars of marble
* set on bases of pure gold.*

His appearance is like Lebanon,
* choice as its cedars.*
His mouth is sweetness itself;
* he is altogether lovely.*
This is my beloved, this is my friend,
* daughters of Jerusalem.*

As we have seen before, the Holy Spirit uses metaphors familiar to the age when this book was written to convey the attributes of the Lord's character. As we dwell deeply on who He is and share these proclamations of His beauty, others are moved, and their lives are changed. It is important that we spend time meditating and writing out our understanding of who He is to us and to the world so that we can share with others. Our journal is a great place to record these impressions.

Verse 16b: He is altogether lovely. This is my lover, and this is my friend, O daughters of Jerusalem.

In summary, He is not only radiant in His majesty, but He humbled Himself to be our friend, and He chose me!

As we read through the written description that the bride gives, ask the real Author, the Holy Spirit, to guide you in your understanding, making note of them in your Bible. Your understanding may deepen as you read these chapters later in your life experience, prompting additions to your notes.

The bride's friends have another question.

Song of Songs 6:1–3 (NIV)

> *Friends*
>
> *Where has your beloved gone,*
>   *most beautiful of women?*
> *Which way did your beloved turn,*
>   *that we may look for him with you?*
>
> *She*
>
> *My beloved has gone down to his garden,*
>   *to the beds of spices,*
> *to browse in the gardens*
>   *and to gather lilies.*
> *I am my beloved's and my beloved is mine;*
>   *he browses among the lilies.*

The bride knows something about her lover that her friends do not. Sometimes, our friends wonder what we know about Jesus that they don't. They are curious about our devotion, our intense love for Him. Hopefully, they say, "We want to know Him like you do. We want what you have."

Her response probably surprises them. Even though she has not seen His presence for a time, she dwells on His beauty. Then she knows where He is.

Of course, He is in his garden. As we look at this beautiful passage with the help of the Spirit, we know that Jesus is in His church and building it. This is the corporate church, the world-wide church. And we also know that Jesus is in each of us, in the inner most heart of us, growing and maturing us, revealing Himself to us.

The beds of spices can mean the different reflections of Jesus's personality in the church, and the lilies speak of purity. The Lord browses among His pure flock and delights in communing with them. Each one of us can experience His presence in the depths of us in a unique way, as we have given over our life to Him. We now can say with certainty, "I am my Beloved's, and He is mine."

THIS WEEK

Have you ever been misunderstood or criticized for your strong love for Christ? How did you respond?

 Write the answer in your JOURNAL.

The words used in the song to describe the maiden's love for the King have spiritual meanings to us who study the book to enhance our appreciation of who Jesus, our King and bridegroom, is.

Using verses 10–16 as a guide, write in your JOURNAL your own description of Jesus as you see Him. Use your own words.

These writings in your JOURNAL are extremely important and should be reviewed in your devotional times. Some are perfect to meditate on as you seek to meet the Lord in your garden. Along with worship music and the Word, these will greatly enhance your experience spiritually and emotionally.

SESSION 7

His Image of Me

How Does the Lord See Me?

Do you realize that your loving gaze overwhelms the Lord? It's true! Our God is a God who has emotions. We know that because we are created in His image and we have emotions. We read of this over and over throughout the Bible's sixty-six chapters. Read the prophetical books where His servants speak forth His sorrow and anguish over His unfaithful people. Hear His mercy and grace in His words of love and forgiveness and restoration promised for these same people.

While it was penned by a man speaking intimate words to his bride, we know that the Holy Spirit breathed into the Song of Songs a spiritual message to the bride of Christ. The Lord purposely speaks to us in words that evoke passion and emotional response, not in a physical sense but in our spirits made alive by His grace. Passion is what makes our giftings desirable and effective to others, inspiring them to partake. It reveals our sincerity. It also speaks of an intimate relationship between the Lord and His bride, a marriage relationship. We will speak more of this in the Epilogue.

What is His image of us? The Bible answers this in many ways. One of them is the next section of the Song, a beautiful description written some three thousand years ago, but it still speaks to us of the way that Jesus looks at us. It is written in poetic and sensual language, which is sure to stir our emotions.

Jesus breaks His silence with the bride that began in Song 5:6. Next, He describes her beauty then makes a most wondrous statement. Our Lover is overwhelmed by our humble faith and love for Him. He is greatly moved, ravished, as some translations say. Our steady gaze of love even in our weakness and brokenness overcomes Him. It is what we were created for, to bring Him pleasure.

Tirzah—known as Isreal's most beautiful city
Jerusalem—chosen to be the place of Solomon's Temple, worship center of the whole world
Troops, banners—victorious over all her enemies
Hair as flock of goats—beautiful to a herding society, Nasserite
Teeth like a flock of newly washed sheep, each with a twin—the redeemed processing, reproducing themselves, fellowshipping and strengthening each other

---

Song of Songs 6:4–9 (niv)

He

You are as beautiful as Tirzah, my darling,
  as lovely as Jerusalem,
  as majestic as troops with banners.
  Turn your eyes from me;
  they overwhelm me.
Your hair is like a flock of goats
  descending from Gilead.
Your teeth are like a flock of sheep
  coming up from the washing.
Each has its twin,
  not one of them is missing.
Your temples behind your veil
  are like the halves of a pomegranate.
Sixty queens there may be,
  and eighty concubines,
  and virgins beyond number;
  but my dove, my perfect one, is unique,
  the only daughter of her mother,
  the favorite of the one who bore her.
The young women saw her and called her blessed;
  the queens and concubines praised her.

Temples (cheeks) as halves of pomegranate—the fruit of an opened pomegranate, bright red, blushing as a modest/pure bride, sweet, hidden life behind a veil

Queens, concubines, virgins—possibly immature Christians or angelic attendants

Dove, perfect one, mother—singleness of heart, walking in the Spirit, mature in the bridal identity, the perfected mature church (as mother), unique; each believer is made righteous but unique as she chooses how deep she will go (Note Matthew 25: 1–13, Revelation 19:7)

What do you think caused the young women (immature) to call the bride blessed? (Song of Songs 6:9)

 Journal about it, and compare to your experiences.

Conversation between the friends and the bride:

6:10: Appearance as the moon, sun, stars—the sun-clad bride (Revelation 12:1), reflecting the Bridegroom's glory.
6:11: The bride goes to her fields of ministry, anxious for the fruit to appear. Royal chariots of my people—the world and its systems

Song of Songs 6:10–13 (niv)

Friends

Who is this that appears like the dawn,
fair as the moon, bright as the sun,
majestic as the stars in procession?

She

I went down to the grove of nut trees
  to look at the new growth in the valley,
to see if the vines had budded
  or the pomegranates were in bloom.
Before I realized it,
  my desire set me among the royal chariots of my people.

6:13: The Lover steps in, noting to the friends that the beloved's ministry is not only to Him, but also to the world.

Mahahaim— Dance before two armies or camps. The bride is single minded and although she lives in a fallen world.

Friends

Come back, come back, O Shulammite;
  come back, come back, that we may gaze on you!

He

Why would you gaze on the Shulammite
  as on the dance of Mahanaim?

The following section contains words that were most likely spoken by the bride's friends. They are very much like what we heard Jesus say to His bride in Song of Solomon 4:1–11. In those verses, what He sees is the perfected, mature bride, the one He created her to be. He begins at her head, giving her a picture of how He sees her as He describes attributes of her character.

In Song of Songs 7:1–5, it is the friends describing the bride as they validate her beauty. The affirmations begin at her feet this time, speaking of characteristics of her ministry, holiness, and fruitfulness. Then in verses 6–9, Jesus continues the description as He delights in seeing His bride. He is truly captivated by her beauty and her fruit.

The passionate words, as Jesus and the friends describe her, are not meant to be sexual. They are a poetic vehicle, however, to arouse *our* passionate love in order to assure us of the ultimate goal of our life here on earth. We are chosen to be the bride of Christ, His resurrected and perfectly mature companion for eternity. The Song fires up our hearts as we proceed to that goal.

Comments to help in spiritual meanings.
Also, be open to the Holy Spirit's wisdom for you in your life.

Sandaled feet—feet shod for evangelism (Ephesians 6:15, Isaiah 52:7)

Legs, thighs—strong and developed through discipline for her walk

Navel—source of nourishment from her mother, grounded in a good foundation, never lacking what is needed

Waist, mound of wheat—mature and pregnant with an abundant harvest, surrounded by lilies, purity, and holiness

Breasts, twins of a gazelle—young with the ability to nurture, a double portion

Neck, ivory tower—her will, which is resolute, but not stubborn, rare, and costly

---

Song of Songs 7:1–9 (niv)

Friends

How beautiful your sandaled feet,
  O prince's daughter!
Your graceful legs are like jewels,
  the work of an artist's hands.
Your navel is a rounded goblet
  that never lacks blended wine.
Your waist is a mound of wheat
  encircled by lilies.
Your breasts are like two fawns,
  like twin fawns of a gazelle.
Your neck is like an ivory tower.
Your eyes are the pools of Heshbon
  by the gate of Bath Rabbim.
Your nose is like the tower of Lebanon
  looking toward Damascus.
Your head crowns you like Mount Carmel.
  Your hair is like royal tapestry;
  the king is held captive by its tresses.

He

How beautiful you are and how pleasing,
  my love, with your delights!
Your stature is like that of the palm,
  and your breasts like clusters of fruit.
I said, "I will climb the palm tree;
  I will take hold of its fruit."
May your breasts be like clusters of grapes on the vine,
  the fragrance of your breath like apples,
and your mouth like the best wine.

She

May the wine go straight to my beloved,
flowing gently over lips and teeth.

Eyes, pools of Heshbon—seeing with spiritual insight as the clear pools in the city of Heshbon Nose, tower of Lebanon—discernment as a protective tower against her enemies

Head, Mount Carmel—powerful thought life, significant in spiritual warfare, crowned by hair (thoughts)
Jesus affirms His Bride vindicating her before the critics.

Stature, palm, breasts, clusters of fruit—she is strong, not easily broken, finding the deep living water, bearing much fruit to nourish many

Jesus vows to take hold of His people, manifesting His presence through them (John 15:5).

Jesus commands her to nurture others in the power of the Holy Spirit, breathing forth His life and fragrance.

Jesus lovingly tells her that her intimate love for Him, her mouth, the kisses of her lips (her words), the breath of the Holy Spirit in her bring the greatest of joys to Him.

The bride returns His words of love, sharing them only with Him.

This is the point of the most important reflection in our journey through the love song between Jesus and His bride. We must stop and consider our own journey toward a more intimate walk with our Lord.

This is where we choose to go on in the adventure of faith to acquire the attributes of His character that will become deeply woven into ours. This is the place where our ministry becomes powerful, not through our own efforts but as a result of our deep relationship in Him. There is no other gate through which to enter. It is the narrow gate spoken of in Matthew 7:13.

The entry is though the garden, our own secret place where only the bridegroom may enter.

Helpmate

"I belong to my Beloved, and His desire is for me" (Song of Songs 7:10).

This is a wonderful place to move on to our partnership in ministry with the Lord, who is our bridegroom. When we begin to trust Him enough to surrender our plans, our will to His, our identity changes. Knowing that we belong to Jesus and giving ownership to Him is the most valued thing in our life. Knowing that His desire is "for me" gives us motivation and courage to step forth in obedience as His helpmate. We are able to overcome doubts and rejections from others. We live a life of sacrificial obedience to Him, not to gain His love but because we already have His love.

READ
John 14:5–17

 In light of what you have just read, paraphrase this passage spoken by Jesus in your own words, and record them in your JOURNAL.

Song of Songs 7:10–13 (NIV)

She

I belong to my beloved,
*   and his desire is for me.*
Come, my beloved, let us go to the countryside,
*   let us spend the night in the villages.*

Let us go early to the vineyards
    to see if the vines have budded,
if their blossoms have opened,
    and if the pomegranates are in bloom—
    there I will give you my love.
The mandrakes send out their fragrance,
    and at our door is every delicacy,
both new and old,
    that I have stored up for you, my beloved.

The bride knows she belongs to the bridegroom. Her will has been surrendered to His, and she is confident in His love. This should be our confidence. It is the Holy Spirit in us that assures us of the bridegroom's love and guidance.

"Filled with the Spirit"—what does that mean? Ephesians 5:18 commands us to be filled with the Spirit. To be continually filled with the Holy Spirit means to continually live under the Holy Spirit's leadership. The New King James Version translates Song of Solomon 7:9b this way:

The wine goes down smoothly for my beloved,
    Moving gently the lips of sleepers.

The bride says that the Word of the Holy Spirit goes into her without resistance because of her love for the bridegroom (Jesus). Wine is often spoken of as the blessing and presence of the Holy Spirit. She desires to be filled with His Spirit that she might be effective in reaching others.

As we intercede for and invite Jesus to go with us to the fields and villages, we are inviting Jesus to go with us as we minister to others. He prepares the way and releases His presence through us with His Holy Spirit. Earlier in Song 6:11, the bride says, "I went down," to check the fruit in her garden. Now in Song 7:11–12, she invites her Beloved to go with her. In order for our ministry to be powerful and passionate, we must first partner with the source of that power and effectiveness—the Holy Spirit. Mandrakes are a symbol of fertility in most cases. As we go to those places near and far, investing in the kingdom of God and ministering to those around us, we are giving our personal love back to Jesus. Our ministry should drip with love for Him, which only inspires more passion, which is continually more and more fulfilling. It is what changes the world.

> *But thanks be to God, who in Christ always leads us in triumphal procession, and through us spreads the fragrance of the knowledge of him everywhere. For we are the aroma of Christ to God among those who are being saved and among those who are perishing, to one a fragrance from death to death, to the other a fragrance from life to life. Who is sufficient for these things? (2 Corinthians 2:14–16, esv)*

 Have you experienced the *diffusing* of the Lord's fragrance in your outreach to others? List at least three times in which you saw this result in other's lives. Record them in your JOURNAL.

Song of Songs 8:1–2 (NIV)

> *If only you were to me like a brother,*
> *who was nursed at my mother's breasts!*
> *Then, if I found you outside,*
> *I would kiss you,*
> *and no one would despise me.*
> *I would lead you*
> *and bring you to my mother's house—*
> *she who has taught me.*
> *I would give you spiced wine to drink,*
> *the nectar of my pomegranates.*

This confusing passage seems to be saying that the bride would like to show her affection to her bridegroom in public without ridicule. It would be more acceptable in that culture to be affectionate in public with her brother than with her beloved. How often would we like to lift our hands and/or voices to praise Jesus or express our love for Him in public or in the church (our mother's house)? As mature believers, we need to walk in love and in God-honoring discernment in our public expressions of love for the One whom our soul loves.

Song of Solomon 8:3–4 (NASB)

> *"Let his left hand be under my head*
> *And his right hand embrace me."*
> *"I want you to swear, O daughters of Jerusalem,*
> *Do not arouse or awaken my love*
> *Until she pleases."*

In answer to His bride's desire to be close to Him at all times, Jesus promises to lay hold of her (Song of Songs 7:8).

- He is always with us in unseen ways (His left hand is under my head), protecting us from harm, leading and guiding us, and providing for our needs and many of our wants.
- He also manifests His presence to us (His right hand embraces me) and allows us to feel His arms around us, as we sense His peace or comfort, as we sense Him walking or sitting next to us or receiving one of His gifts of the Spirit to give to another. We feel our heart being tenderized by His tender hand, bringing purity to our motives and feeling the joy of His love for us.
- In verse 4, it seems to be the Holy Spirit reminding those who do not share this closeness with the bridegroom that they should not interfere. It is the bride who enters into

this intimacy and joy. It is her decision to respond to the leadings of God in her life.

So the King will greatly desire your beauty;
Because He is your Lord, worship Him.
(Psalm 45:11, NKJV)

The Lord your God in your midst,
The Mighty One, will save;
He will rejoice over you with gladness,
He will quiet you with His love
He will rejoice over you with singing.

Zephaniah 3:17 (NKJV)

THIS WEEK

Take time each day to read through Song of Songs 7:1–9.

Ask the Holy Spirit to teach you what He wants you to learn. Listen for His voice as you read and meditate.

Consider each attribute of the bride and its development in you. Remember, there is no condemnation for those who are in Christ Jesus (Rom. 8:1) as you examine truthfully your own character and ministry. Do you need to surrender *your* will in some area?

Most important of all, converse with your bridegroom as you go through this process. It is He who makes you beautiful.

 Write in your JOURNAL what you feel about these two verses:

As the Father has loved me, so have I loved you. Now remain in my love. (John 15:9, NIV)

Now hope does not disappoint, because the love of God has been poured out in our hearts by the Holy Spirit who was given to us. (Romans 5:5, NKJV)

Have an honest conversation with the Lord about what you wrote.

SESSION 8

The Seal

Meet Me in morning stillness, while the earth is fresh with the dew of My Presence. Worship Me in the beauty of holiness. Sing love songs to My holy Name. As you give yourself to Me, My Spirit swells within you till you are flooded with divine Presence. The world's way of pursuing riches is grasping and hoarding. You attain My riches by letting go and giving. The more you give yourself to Me and My ways, the more I fill you with inexpressible, heavenly Joy.

—Sarah Young (Jesus Calling, May 4)

We cannot love God without the Spirit's supernatural help enabling us to love Him with our whole heart, mind, and strength. It takes God to love God. While the Song of Songs is a love song describing the love between King Solomon and his bride, it is also an allegory describing the spiritual truths in the relationship between King Jesus and His bride. Over three thousand years, God's people have used it to lead them into a greater and more passionate love relationship with God.

It progresses from the initial response of the bride to His wooing of her through the growth of trust, faith, and revelation of who He is to the surrendering of her life into His hands. "I belong to my Beloved, and His desire is for me" (Song of Songs 7:10). At this point in her relationship with the Lord, the bride eagerly awaits those times of intimacy with Him as she communes with Him, sharing her heart and longing to share His. She remembers the beginning of this relationship with fondness and thankfulness for those who have guided her along her journey. However, the deep commitments to go even deeper are hers as she responds to her Lover, the Lover of our soul. She desires to know Him even more.

We start this session with another conversation between the bride and those friends who are watching her journey with much interest. In our walk with Christ, we are continually being observed and often judged by others who wish to emulate us or to criticize us for our devotion or our theology. One of the marks of maturity is that we are able to "discern what is best" (Philippians 1:10), having faith that the Holy Spirit is leading us into truth and righteousness.

Song of Solomon 8:5–7 (NKJV)

> *Who is this coming up from the wilderness,*
> *Leaning upon her beloved?*

He

I awakened you under the apple tree.
There your mother brought you forth;
There she who bore you brought you forth.

Set me as a seal upon your heart,
As a seal upon your arm;
For love is as strong as death,
Jealousy as cruel as the grave;
Its flames are flames of fire,
A most vehement flame.

Many waters cannot quench love,
Nor can the floods drown it.
If a man would give for love
All the wealth of his house,
It would be utterly despised.

We ascend from the wilderness of trials, tribulations, and testing knowing God is the source of our victory. Our faith perfected, we are able to die more and more to self (our own plans, desires, reasoning) and lean on our bridegroom, trusting our life into His arms of love.

In the Song, Jesus reminds His bride that it was He who awakened her love by His love. As she responds, He raises her up, preparing her to spend eternity with Him.

This kind of passionate and powerful love will not allow any areas of darkness to escape its grasp. Jesus jealously wants all of us. This seal is demanding, causing us to die to our own will and desires. The Holy Spirit is the all-consuming fire and the living flame of love that baptizes us with His fiery love.

The love that Jesus offers us, sealing it on our heart (emotions) and our arm (actions), is what purifies and changes us. It is the highest thing that God will give the human spirit in this age. In ancient times, a lump of hot wax was pressed onto an important document or item, stamped with the stamp of a king or other important official. It permanently assured the validity of the document and that it had not been seen or violated in any way. This is a picture of the eternal guarantee of God's love and protection.

The waters of sin and pressures cannot quench our love or drown His. There is nothing more powerful or desirable. Jesus eagerly awaits for us to respond to this love by putting on the new man. It is an act of our will even though we may not understand exactly what that means. It is a response made in faith.

> **READ**
> Luke 3:16, Acts 2:3, Colossians 3:10, Ephesians 4:24

What do these verses say about the ways in which we are changed by God in our walk with Him?

How do they relate to the Bridal relationship with Jesus?

 Write about this and your experiences in your JOURNAL.

The Bride's Intercession for the Church

The invitation by Jesus to enter into His very personal and passionate love is open to all in the Church. In fact, God desires that all men might know His love (John 3:16). Once we are born again by faith in our redemption by His own life and blood, we begin to respond in the power of the Holy Spirit to His love and discipline.

"If right from the start a believer being 'in Christ...a new creation' (2 Corinthians. 5:17) is a wonder to behold, how will Christ's bride appear when she is 'like Him' and 'shall see Him as He is' (1 John 3:2)?" (*Song of Songs*, Richard Brooks).

In this love song to the Church, the maiden grows in her response until she becomes a bride filled with the fiery love of

God. In her maturity, she understands who she is in Christ and desires, as does her bridegroom, that all might grow and mature. Her intercession to her bridegroom for these "young ones" is immensely important as well as her example, and she joins Him in this mature partnership. We are called to intercede for and set a good example to these immature believers and to be concerned for the spiritual condition of others.

This short passage is often attributed to *friends* or *brothers* of the bride. However, many believe it is the conversation between the bride and her bridegroom. In other words, she intercedes for others who remain as babes in Christ. She and her bridegroom are a team, both pouring out His love on these immature believers and encouraging them to respond.

Song of Songs 8:8–10 (NIV)

She

We have a little sister,
* and her breasts are not yet grown.*
What shall we do for our sister
* on the day she is spoken for?*
If she is a wall,
* we will build towers of silver on her.*
If she is a door,
* we will enclose her with panels of cedar.*

I am a wall,
* and my breasts are like towers.*
Thus I have become in his eyes
* like one bringing contentment.*

The Bride's Confidence in Who She Is
Interpretation helps

Wall—a wall of protection, confident in Jesus's life in her to help others

Breasts like towers—the ability to nurture others provided by the power of the Holy Spirit

The bride finds great peace and contentment in God's plan for her life. She also enjoys living before His eyes, enjoying a radiant confidence in her walk with Jesus.

READ
Mark 10:28–31; John 15:8, 16; 1 Corinthians 3:11–15;
2 Corinthians 5:10; Romans 14:12

 Write down at least two things you learn from these passages for the Church in your JOURNAL.

Verses 11 and 12 of the eighth chapter speak to us of the responsibility of the bride as she cultivates her vineyard, a gift from her bridegroom. As you have discovered in Paul's letters to his converts, we will be held accountable for our fruitfulness. Our love for Jesus must also result in love for one another if it is genuine.

Baal Hamon cannot be identified as a specific place but speaks to us of a very large vineyard (multitudes of nations), which has been entrusted to us as Jesus's bride. Each believer is given a certain stewardship in His vineyard. A thousand shekels represents a complete or full payment, speaking to us of the full potential of our love and ministry to others, given back to God for His glory.

However, Jesus, as our bridegroom, is very generous with His blessings, joy, and peace as He bestows them upon us in return. In verse 12, the bride gives her full payment to her bridegroom and is given back her own reward as the one who tends its fruit. We will each receive our reward in eternity on the last day.

Song of Songs 8:11–13 (NIV)

> *Solomon had a vineyard in Baal Hamon;*
>   *he let out his vineyard to tenants.*
> *Each was to bring for its fruit*
>   *a thousand shekels of silver.*
> *But my own vineyard is mine to give;*
>   *the thousand shekels are for you, Solomon,*
>   *and two hundred are for those who tend its fruit.*

He

> *You who dwell in the gardens*
>   *with friends in attendance,*
>   *let me hear your voice!*

Just as the bride is individually in Jesus's garden (Song of Songs 5:1), the church herself as a whole is Christ's garden. In both cases, this is where I must dwell as long as I am on this earth. As His garden (or vineyard), I bring great joy to Him as He hears my voice in worship, intercession, teaching, and evangelism. It is in His garden (my heart) that we commune and grow closer together. It is where I grow in my knowledge of Him as He reveals more and more of Himself to me. It is where He prunes out the dead and useless things in my life in order that I may grow stronger and more fruitful.

On the other hand, the church is also His garden or vineyard. It reaches to the multitudes of the nations. Jesus leases out His vineyard to His bride knowing she would keep it for Him. Each believer is given a certain stewardship in His vineyard. You may not have a title, but you can begin by serving others, loving them, encouraging them, and witnessing to them.

In Matthew 21:33–44, Jesus tells a parable about a landowner who planted a vineyard, built a tower, and leased it to keepers then went into a far country. This speaks of the time when Jesus, as the landowner, has gone and left His vineyard for us to care for in partnership with Him. In Luke 12:42–48, He gives another example of what He expects from those to whom He has leased out His vineyard. In the Song, the King demands one thousand shekels of silver (one thousand is a Biblical number of completion or fullness) from each tenant at harvest time. In the same sense, Jesus demands a full measure of our efforts of what was entrusted to us when we stand before Him on judgment day.

This becomes our individual vineyard. The bride in the Song is confident that she will give Jesus all that He expects from her as she declares that the one thousand shekels are for Him, and she will share a portion with all who minister with her. This speaks of the glory which, when given to the Father, shines back on us. Paul spoke similar words when he said, *"Not that I seek the gift, but I seek the fruit that abounds to your account" (Philippians 4:17, nkjv).*

The last words of the King to the bride commend her effectiveness in serving the church. She has taught others to hear His voice and has lived a life that speaks of their close relationship. Now He calls her again to fervent worship and intercession. Her voice, which was sweet to Him in her immaturity (Song 2:14), is now even sweeter as they are joined in this mature and holy union.

Song of Songs 8:14 (NIV)

She

Come away, my beloved,
    and be like a gazelle
or like a young stag
    on the spice-laden mountains.

Responding immediately to Jesus's exhortation, the bride flies to Jesus. As I hear His voice and in my longing to see His face and look into His eyes, I cry out to Him to "Come near me in intimacy," "Come, bring revival to the world," and "Come and meet me in the sky." While I am here on this earth, I long for His continued presence spiritually to know Him more and more completely in every way. Even more, my heart cries out for His second coming where I will see my bridegroom face-to-face, be changed into His image, and attend the marriage supper of the Lamb as His wife, the bride for eternity. My cry is "Come quickly, Lord Jesus!" (Revelation. 22:20).

"It is the consistent testimony of Scripture that the Lord Jesus Christ will come again—personally, visibly and gloriously. He will come in His Father's glory, on the clouds of heaven, in the company of the angels, and at the sound of a trumpet. Here at the end of the Song, this is what Christ looks forward to as His joyous prospect, and this is what His church looks forward to as her spiritual horizon—bridegroom and bride together. Yet this is not only how the Song of Songs ends. For how does the whole of Scripture end? In exactly the same way (Rev. 22:20), where the Lord Jesus Christ utters the precious words, 'Surely, I am coming quickly,' and His bride responds (how else?), 'Amen. Even so, come, Lord Jesus!'" (Richard Brooks, *Song of Songs*)

> *And the Spirit and the bride say, "Come!" And let him who hears say, "Come!" And let him who thirsts come. Whoever desires, let him take the water of life freely.*
>
> *He who testifies to these things says, "Surely I am coming quickly."*
>
> *Amen. Even so, come, Lord Jesus! (Revelation 22:17, 20)*

THIS WEEK

and on and on

Read the epilogue and look up the scriptures mentioned there.

Read the Song of Solomon often, especially when you feel your need to feel His love.

Read the Song of Solomon often, when you need to stir up your love for Jesus.

 Write in and reread your JOURNAL frequently, reminding yourself of where you have been and where you are going.

EPILOGUE

The last few words of the Song of Solomon project a picture of the bride standing on a small lush hill, with her back to us and her arm raised in a wave as she looks into the sunset. We might see, silhouetted in the bright orange light of the beautiful sunset, her bridegroom riding off on His horse, waving back at her. We are left with the feeling of: "What next? This can't be all there is. It can't be the end!" And of course, it is not.

It is often said of the Bible that the Old Testament is the New Testament *concealed* and the New Testament is the Old Testament *revealed*. And I think that fits the Song so well. The story of the bridegroom God is concealed in the Old Testament in the *Song of Songs*, in the Psalms of David, and in the prophecies of many of the Old Testament prophets. Now we must go to the New Testament to see it revealed. But they cannot be separated.

The prophets of the Old Testament foresaw this story although they did not understand it. They even saw things beyond the suffering and death and the resurrection of the bridegroom. They saw the bridegroom King, His second coming as King of Kings. However, we still don't have a clear picture of what and when that will be manifested.

So let's review what we do know through the help of the Holy Spirit.

- Before creation, the Father, Son, and Holy Spirit had a plan. The plan involved flesh and blood humans, made in Their image, who would share fellowship with Them and partnership with Them in taking dominion over the earth.
- Because one of the gifts of God to these humans is a free will, giving them a choice to receive and respond to His plan, we know that Adam and Eve made the wrong choice, separating them from their Creator. God provided them with a way to temporarily approach Him as He gave them the Law and the whole system of animal sacrifices.
- The relationship that is longed for by the Creator is one that is best described by His references to His people being His wife or His bride because it is in the mutual trust, respect, and emotional love found in a godly, committed marriage.
- The next step in this plan was the manifested Son in flesh and blood, who revealed to the created ones what God is like. His purpose was also to, in a sense, pay the "bride price" for His bride, His very life for her sin. Those who would by faith receive this wondrous and priceless gift receive the invitation to be His bride for eternity, to be in fellowship again with God. He would give His life for

her, be raised from the dead, reveal His resurrected flesh to many, and ascend into heaven to sit with His Father on the throne, interceding for His bride as she tells the world of this wondrous Savior and ministering to and inviting them to also believe and receive all that He promises.

- Jesus, the Son of God, the Bridegroom, also taught specifically that this was not the end. Although He would ascend into heaven, He left them Himself, in spiritual form as the Holy Spirit, who would lead them into all truth, comfort them, empower and enable them. The Spirit would reveal the depth of His love for them and His plans to return as the bridegroom coming for His bride.

Most of us believe that current events seem to be indicating that the prophecies of the Old Testament and Jesus, Himself, are close to being fulfilled for the next great event in this plan. In Revelation, the one prophetical book of the New Testament, John, the only remaining original disciple at this point in history writes of the many mysterious things He is shone. He struggles to understand them just as we do. But we have the Holy Spirit. The Spirit seems to be nudging the Church, the bride, to get in line, to be ready.

One of the themes, most assuredly, is the renewed emphasis on the only commandment in the New Testament given to us when Jesus was on earth.

Jesus replied: "'Love the Lord your God with all your heart and with all your soul and with all your mind.'
This is the first and greatest commandment.
And the second is like it: 'Love your neighbor as yourself.'
All the Law and the Prophets hang on these two commandments."

—Matthew 22:37–40

Jesus is calling us to love Him with all our heart, soul, and mind. Isn't this what the whole theme of the Song of Solomon is? That is why this study is so important. Loving our neighbor comes after we love the Lord with total abandonment. To reverse the order results in discouragement and burnout, often leading to deception and losing our faith. The power to love people the way that Jesus did comes from Him, from a bridal relationship with Him. We also must allow that love to seal us to Him in order that we might endure what may come and overcome.

But all that does not answer our lovesick longing for Him to manifest Himself to us again, to come again, to bring us to Himself, and to consummate the marriage between us. This consummation, although we don't fully understand it, will involve our instantaneous transformation.

> *For the Lord himself will come down from heaven, with a loud command, with the voice of the archangel and with the trumpet call of God, and the dead in Christ will rise first. (1 Thessalonians 4:16, NIV)*

> *But our citizenship is in heaven. And we eagerly await a Savior from there, the Lord Jesus Christ, who, by the power that enables him to bring everything under his control, will transform our lowly bodies so that they will be like his glorious body. (Philippians 3:20–21, NIV)*

> *Listen, I tell you a mystery: We will not all sleep, but we will all be changed—in a flash, in the twinkling of an eye, at the last trumpet. For the trumpet will sound, the dead will be raised imperishable, and we will be changed. (1 Corinthians 15:51–52, NIV)*

This transformation prepares us to be the *helpmate* of God— the totally submitted bride who is endowed with all the perfection needed to fulfill that role. This is not just a collective relationship but an intensely personal and individual joining of all that we are in our new perfection with Jesus, the bridegroom. At the same time, in this realm of no time restraints, Jesus is able to spend as much time with each of us as we desire and somehow to form us all into a completely able bride for the adventure of eternity.

We do know from Revelation that the wedding supper of the Lamb is next on the schedule. It's helpful to realize that the revelation to John uses familiar terms to him such as "wedding supper" and "the Lamb." In ancient times, even up till now in some places of the world, the bridegroom and bride go through some sort of public ceremony and then are allowed to go to privacy to consummate their marriage while the wedding supper, the celebration, continues on, sometimes for days. After the consummation, the bride and groom, legally married now, join the celebration.

What an incredible picture this gives us of the awaiting event when Jesus comes again to collect His bride. The consummation is the transformation of the bride who totally yields all that she is to her bridegroom, allowing Him to make Himself known to her and to bring her (in the twinkling of an eye) to the perfection which He, the Father, and the Holy Spirit had originally planned for her. Of course, this is not a sexual union, a special but totally inadequate part of earthly marriage. It is not gender specific. Men and women alike are called to this marvelous love relationship that results in the perfection that we all long to find in ourselves.

And more importantly, we can look into our Savior's eyes. We can touch the face of our bridegroom, kneel at His feet, and look up into His smile. We can see Him as we go together to accomplish His will. I believe that this will include His will on earth, to totally conquer Satan and reign over the kingdoms of this world. The details of all this are not clear, and there are many different interpretations, but this we know. We will be at His side.

Then I heard what sounded like a great multitude, like the roar
of rushing waters and like loud peals of thunder, shouting:

"Hallelujah!
For our Lord God Almighty reigns.
Let us rejoice and be glad and give him glory!
For the wedding of the Lamb has come,
And his bride has made herself ready.
Fine linen, bright and clean, was given her to wear."
(Fine linen stands for the righteous acts of the saints.)

—Revelation 19:6–8

I saw the Holy City, the new Jerusalem, coming down out of
heaven from God, prepared as a bride beautifully dressed for
her husband. One of the seven angels who had the seven bowls
full of the seven last plagues came and said to me, "Come, I will
show you the bride, the wife of the Lamb."

—Revelation 21:2, 9

One last thing, we also do not know exactly when all this will happen in the life of the church here on earth. There are again many interpretations. As for me, the author, it is enough to know these things that I have written above. However, Jesus warned us to be aware of the signs of the time to not be ignorant of the prophecies surrounding these end-time events. He meant for us to listen—ourselves—to the Holy Spirit as He leads and directs us in our preparations. He is faithful to do so; however, that requires us to grow closer to Him, to take the time, to sacrifice our own will sometimes, and to be open to the truth that He whispers in our spiritual ears. It requires us to grow strong, wise, and able to follow Him no matter what lies ahead. It requires us to respond to His passionate love for us to love Him with all our heart, with all our soul, and with all our mind.

Discussion:

What does it really mean: "Love the Lord, your God, with all your *heart*, with all your *soul*, with all your *mind*?"

What do you think this *transformation* will look like?

How does the bride make herself ready for the wedding?

Do you think there will be different responses to this preparation of the bride?

How will these differences affect the individual believer in his/her experience in eternity?

Note: there are no incorrect answers to these questions. However, it is important to give these things some thought and perhaps more study in the Bible. The Holy Spirit guides us into all Truth even when the *true* answer may be "Wait."

JOURNAL

I came to believe Jesus is my Lord & Savior in my 70th year. I've always known Jesus. But it's just since 2016 that the depth of his commitment finally struck me. Really understood salvation.

It is nearly impossible to come to God like a breadcrumb. He is so omnipotent & I am barely a speck of dust. The prize of his certainly knowing & loving me is unimaginable. I will pray for his gift. Today I have prayed &

prayed to my spiritual
father, so needing his
love and fatherly presence.
His love sustains me today.
I am an emotional wreck.
Debbie left, I feel so alone.
Calling deep has helped me.
be sane. I'm trying to give
love & kindness in HIS
spirit. Thank you, AMEN.
I feel so unworthy. It's
just so sad. But I know
God loves me,

Sept. 8-17
        I seek to grow in my love
for the lord because my soul
is empty. I now realize the
only way to fill it is to
become closer to God. No
thing on this earth can
fill the emptiness
    I believe Jesus sees me as
a child of God. Flawed &
sinful but with hope for
me to work for beauty

and become his Bride,

Little Foxes:
Anger
Self-pity
Gossip
Speaking ill of others
& TOH —
All are things I can Control